Healing at Home

A guidebook for cleansing and detoxification with Ayurveda and Naturopathy

by Dr. Nibodhi Haas

Mata Amritanandamayi Center, San Ramon
California, United States

Healing at Home
By Dr. Nibodhi Haas
A guidebook for cleansing and detoxification
with Ayurveda and Naturopathy

Published by:
Mata Amritanandamayi Center
P.O. Box 613
San Ramon, CA 94583
United States

In India:
www.amritapuri.org
inform@amritapuri.org

In Europe:
www.amma-europe.org

In US:
www.amma.org

Disclaimer: All material in this book is provided solely for
informational or educational purposes. The instructions and
advice presented are in no way intended as medical advice or as
a substitute for medical counseling. The information should be
used in conjunction with the guidance and care of a physician.
Consult a physician before beginning any health program. A
physician should be aware of any and all medical conditions that
you may have as well as the medications and supplements you
take.

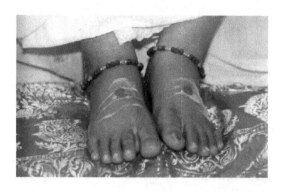

Offerings

I offer this book, my thoughts, my words, my actions,
and my life at the sacred Lotus Feet of my beloved
Satguru Sri Mata Amritanandamayi Devi.

Any omissions in this text are entirely the responsibility
of the author. All truth and benefit that might be received
from this book is solely due to the Guru's grace.

Om Asato Ma Sat Gamaya
Tamaso Ma Jyotir Gamaya
Mrtyor Ma Amrtam Gamaya

Lead us from Untruth to Truth,
Darkness to Light,
Death to Immortality.

Om Lokah Samastah Sukhino Bhavantu

May all beings in all the worlds be happy.

Om Shanti Shanti Shanti

May there be peace, peace, peace. May peace prevail.

Contents

Sri Mata Amritanandamayi Devi   9

Part 1.   Cleansing and Detoxification   11

Chapter 1.   Shodhana: The Need for Detoxification   12

Where Do Toxins Come From?   13
Manas Shodhana (Mental Purification)   14
Stress-Related Diseases   16
Types of Stress   17
When To Do an Internal At-home Cleanse   20
The 15 Most Common Signs Your Body Needs Cleansing   20
The Need to Cleanse the Lymphatic System   21

Chapter 2.   What is Ayurveda?   24

Aspects Unique to Ayurveda   26

Chapter 3.   Overview of 5-35 Day Ayurvedic Home Cleanse   27

Daily Regimen (Dinacharya)   27
Ahara (Food/Diet Therapy)   28

Chapter 4.   Dinacharya (Daily Regime)   30

Waking & Sleeping with the Natural Cycles   30
Oral Hygiene   31
Abhyanga (Application of Oil)   32
Exercise   33
Basic Surya Namaskar Mantra and Instruction   34
Practical Benefits of Surya Namaskar   37
Nasya – Nasal Drops   39
Meditation   40
Mantra As Meditation   43
Pranayama   50

Bedtime, Bath, And Massage		52

Chapter 5.   Supplements   54

Chapter 6.   Ahara (Meal Planning/Food Therapy)   60

Organic Food   61
Food as Prayer   63
Meal Plan One: Kichari Only   64
Meal Plan Two: Kichari with Vegetables   65

Chapter 7.   Shodhana (Purification)   69

Hydration   69
Swedhana (Sweating)   70
Virechan (Intestinal Purgation)Day 5 Intestinal Purgation   72
Basti (Enemas) – Caring for Your Colon   73

Chapter 8.   Completing the Cleanse and Re-Integrating   80

Chapter 9.   What is Naturopathy?   83

Chapter 10.   Overview of 5-35 Day Naturopathic Home Cleanse   86

Daily Regimen (Dinacharya)   86
Purification Supplements   88
Flushing Out the Toxins   88

Chapter 11.   Naturopathic Meal Plans   90

Meal Plan One   91
Meal Plan Two   93
Meal Plan Three   95
Juice!   95
Deep DivecDetox   95
Daily Schedule   97
Atma Vicharya (Self-Inquiry)   99

Chapter 12.   Naturopathic Heavy Metal Detox   101

Daily Routine   101

Chapter 13. The Recipes   108
  Vegetable Dishes   112
  Salads   112
  Soups   118
  Vegetables   122

Part 2. Maintaining Health and Consciousness 133

Chapter 14. The Doshas, Gunas, Ojas, Tejas, and Prana
                                                        134
  Vata   137
  Pitta   139
  Kapha   141
  The Three Gunas   142
  Sattva   144
  Rajas   144
  Tamas   145
  Ojas, Tejas, Prana   148
  Ojas   149
  Tejas   150
  Prana   151
  Diet, Doshas, and Gunas   153

Chapter 15. The Ayurvedic Diet: Food as Medicine   155
  Six Types of Nutritional Imbalances   158
  Benefits of a Sattvic Diet   159
  Food-Combining Guidelines   160
  The Six Tastes   161
  Balancing the Diet   163
  Vata-Balancing Diet   164
  Pitta-Balancing Diet   166
  Kapha-Balancing Diet   168

Chapter 16.   Self-Examination and Food Charts   171

   Prakriti – Your Individual Constitution   171
   Subdosha Charts   173
   Three Gunas Constitutional Chart   176
   Food Charts   178

Chapter 17.   The Real Goal of Life   199

   The Four Goals of Life   200
   Eco-Dharma   203

Sri Mata Amritanandamayi Devi

*The world should know that a life dedicated to selfless love
and service is possible. Love is our true essence. Love has
no limitations of caste, religion, race or nationality. We
are all beads strung together on the same thread of love.*

~ Amma

Through Her extraordinary acts of love and self-sacrifice, Mata Amritanandamayi, or Amma (Mother) as She is commonly known, has endeared Herself to millions of people around the world. Tenderly caressing everyone who comes to Her, holding them close to Her heart in a loving embrace, Amma shares boundless love with all, regardless of their beliefs, who they are, or why they have come to Her. In this simple yet powerful way, Amma is transforming the lives of countless people, helping their hearts to blossom, one embrace at a time. In the past 40 years, Amma has physically hugged more than forty million people from all parts of the world.

Her tireless dedication to uplifting others has inspired a vast network of charitable activities through which people are discovering the peace that comes from selflessly serving others.

Amma's teachings are universal. Whenever She is asked about her religion, She replies that Her religion is Love. She does not ask anyone to believe in God or to change their faith, but only to inquire into their own real nature and to believe in themselves.

Among the wide array of charitable projects that have been inspired by Amma are free homes for the poor, worldwide disaster relief work, an orphanage, free food, medicine, and pensions for destitute women, sponsored weddings for the poor, free legal aid, prisoners welfare programs, extensive healthcare programs that

9

include multi-specialty hospitals and medical camps that offer free healthcare to the poor, and many schools, colleges, and educational programs.

For more information on Amma's charitable activities, please visit:

www.embracingtheworld.org
www.amritapuri.org
www.amma.org

Part 1

Cleansing and Detoxification

1

Shodhana: The Need for Detoxification

To care for the body is a duty; otherwise the mind will not be strong and clear.

~ Buddha

Shodhana is a Sanskrit word meaning "cleaning" or "purifying." In Ayurveda, shodhana is a unique process of internal and external purification that purifies and detoxifies the human body. Shodhana treatment aims at removing factors of somatic and psychosomatic diseases. It is also used to increase the effects of various kinds of substances and drugs used in Ayurvedic medicine with the goal of reducing their toxic contents and effects, as well as enhancing their therapeutic properties. Shodhana aims for complete balancing of the unbalanced *doshas* and the purification of the channels of circulation. Shodhana includes the process of *panchakarma* (five actions) that employs *vamana* (therapeutic vomiting), *virechana* (stomach and purgation of the gastrointestinal tract), *basti* (decoction and/or oil enemas), and *nasya* (applying medicated oil and purification of the nose). According to the great Ayurveda physician Sushruta, the fifth purification in panchakarma is known as *Rakta Mokashana*. This is a procedure for removing vitiated blood from the body.

The environment today is vastly different from the environment of our ancestors. Over the last 200 years, an overwhelming number of chemicals have been introduced to our food, air, and water. Pollutants are present in both our indoor and outdoor environments.

Many of these chemicals have not been tested for safety, are known to be toxic, or are assumed to be safe since they are present in low concentrations. However, if many low-concentration pollutants are present, they may collectively yield a serious negative effect on our health.

There are literally thousands of known human-made toxins in our environment. Many of these chemicals are endocrine disruptors that lead to serious illnesses such as autoimmune disorders and cancers, which are rapidly increasing. These chemicals are also associated with many chronic diseases, including liver and kidney disease, coronary artery disease, and diabetes.

The body has a built-in system for recognizing, breaking down, and eliminating toxic waste material. It does this through a specialized network of enzymes, transporters, eliminatory pathways, and physical expulsion. It is not equipped to remove the onslaught of toxins we experience in today's world. These toxins can get stuck in the liver, lymphatic system, and digestive tract, overwhelming the body's natural detoxification pathways. When these mechanisms are blocked or fail, the body becomes auto-intoxicated and disease follows.

Where Do Toxins Come From?

Environmental toxins: These toxins come from industrialized places where there are cars, water and air pollution, radiation, pesticides, and herbicides. They are also in household cleaning products, hair sprays, perfumes, and make-up, and even the material used to build and maintain our homes.

Lifestyle toxins: Lifestyle toxins come from chemicals that we put into our bodies like sugar, prescription drugs, processed foods, alcohol, caffeine, and tobacco.

Metabolic toxins: When our bodies improperly break down proteins, sugars, and fats, they produce toxic waste by-products. This is called malabsorption, and it's a primary cause of toxicity and the start of the disease process. Also, when a diet does not contain enough nutrients or properly balanced nutrients, toxins build up in the body.

Intestinal microbes: The gastrointestinal tract is filled with yeast and bacteria that support the body's digestive process. When there is an excess growth of unhealthy bacteria in the intestinal tract, toxins enter the bloodstream, which results in various health conditions.

Emotional toxins: Stress, fear, ACEs (Adverse Childhood Experiences), or any traumatic event can affect the immune, nervous, and hormonal systems, which then affect your body's detoxification pathways.

Manas Shodhana (Mental Purification)

Manas is the mind bound by time and space, name and form. It operates through the world of the senses. As such, the mind is both an organ of sensation and of action. The senses receive numerous impressions from the external world. The mind then accepts the senses, and the impressions are perceived and formulated into concepts. The mind thinks, the intellect determines, and the ego becomes conscious and projects itself back onto the world. The mind has the ability to discriminate and create a peaceful, *sattvic* existence. It is also necessary for actions in the material world to occur. There is a great saying: "The mind makes a horrible master, but an excellent servant."

Humanity has always tried to attain peace and happiness through any and all available means. Nowadays, the need to attain mental peace is more urgent due to the tremendous increase in stress from modern life, which is the root cause of many diseases. Rapid industrialization, urban crowding, too much competition, and excessive hurry are some of the major contributing factors leading to stress. Worries about physical security and economic difficulties also take a drastic toll on health and longevity.

The body reacts to physical or emotional stress by increasing the production of hormones such as cortisol and epinephrine. These hormones elevate the heart rate, blood pressure, and metabolism to help the body react quickly to a stressful situation. In effect, the body in a state of stress creates extra energy to protect itself. This process is the body's natural "fight or flight" mechanism, and it is incredibly useful in dangerous situations.

Unfortunately, the type of stress experienced by most people today is not a fleeting occurrence in a harmful situation, but an ongoing state that many accept as a natural part of daily life. In fact, many people are unaware of how stressed out they really are. Because the extra energy produced by the body under stress cannot be destroyed, it creates imbalance within the whole body-mind system. This energy creates inflammation and leads to disease.

At first, chronic stress can manifest as irritability, nervousness, sleeplessness, headaches, and constipation. If these symptoms are not addressed, the person may manifest new symptoms such as heart/vein palpitations or raised/high blood pressure. If stress is allowed to continue even further, one may develop psychosomatic disorders such as hypertension, ulcerative colitis, ischemic heart disease, peptic ulcers, diabetes mellitus, bronchial asthma, migraines, and rheumatoid arthritis.

Stress also contributes to numerous skin conditions such as psoriasis, eczema, hives, and acne. It can also trigger asthma attacks. Other common manifestations of stress include disturbances of the digestive system, such as stomach aches and diarrhea. Because chronic stress depletes and weakens the immune system, it renders one more susceptible to colds and other infections.

Chronic stress creates continuously high levels of cortisol, leading to an increase in appetite and thus weight gain. Weight gain puts one at serious risk for many diseases, especially those of the heart. Cortisol also raises the heart rate, increases blood pressure, and elevates blood lipid (cholesterol and triglyceride) levels, all of which makes one more susceptible to heart attacks and strokes.

At the emotional level, when the body remains in a constant fight-or-flight response, one experiences increased feelings of anxiety, helplessness, and depression. It's unsurprising that chronic stress has been linked with severe depression.

Stress-Related Diseases

The American Psychological Association states that 43% of all adults suffer adverse health effects from stress, and 75–90% of all physician office visits are for stress-related ailments. Chronic stress is linked to six leading causes of death: heart disease, cancer, lung disorders, diabetes, cirrhosis of the liver, and suicide.

Here is a partial list of conditions known to be directly triggered by stress. This is not a complete list of all stress-related illnesses. Remember, these diseases are not caused solely by stress, but stress is one of the major causes of their onset.

- Alcoholism
- Asthma
- Auto-immune disorders
- Bronchitis
- Cancer
- Cirrhosis
- Peptic ulcers
- Depression: acute and chronic
- Diabetes
- Fatigue
- Headaches: tension and migraine
- Impaired immune function
- Indigestion
- Insomnia
- Irritable Bowel Syndrome
- Ischemic Heart Disease
- Psychoneurosis
- Sexual dysfunction: infertility, impotency, sterility, etc.

- Skin diseases: eczema, psoriasis, dermatitis, etc.
- Stomatitis
- Smoking
- Violence

Types of Stress

Identifying stress and becoming aware of its effects on our lives is the single most important aspect of managing stress. There are many sources and types of stress. They include external, internal, mental, and emotional stress. External stressors include adverse physical conditions such as exposure to extreme temperatures of hot and cold, or a drastic change in temperature. Another common external stressor is exposure to unhealthy psychological environments such as unpleasant working conditions, school pressures, unhealthy relationships, or having to meet difficult work deadlines. Other external stressors include major traumatic life events, such as the death of a loved one, job loss, demotion/promotion, or the ending of a relationship.

Internal stressors can be physical, like bodily infections or exposure to ongoing or unbearable pain. Many factors such as lifestyle choices, negative thoughts, mental rigidity, and self-imposed ideals can create stress. Lifestyle choices include diet, intake of drugs/alcohol/stimulants, sleeping patterns, daily schedules, and relationships. Negative thoughts include self-doubt, pessimism, self-criticism, over-analyzing, and worrying. Mental rigidity includes unrealistic expectations about ourselves, life, and the situations we encounter. It also includes taking things personally, exaggeration, inflexible thinking, and unnecessary self-limitations. Self-imposed idealism includes being a perfectionist or workaholic, and trying to please everyone all of the time.

Stress is also created when we are not in harmony with nature and living a balanced way of life. When one strives too hard to achieve this balance, harmony is disturbed and stress is the result.

This outcome is especially true for those excessively seeking pleasure and wealth. Too often, these desires are the primary motivations in life because one wrongly thinks they are the source of lasting happiness. These desires can be used for spiritual growth if harnessed correctly. With awareness, the desire to find a source of lasting happiness can lead us to look within, meditate, and reflect on the true nature of things.

Mental stress, according to Ayurveda, is caused by an overuse or wrong use of the mental faculties. If you perform intense mental work for many hours a day, or if you work long hours on a computer, that can cause an imbalance in *prana vata*, the mind-body conductor responsible for brain activity, energy, and the mind. The first symptom of prana vata imbalance is losing the ability to cope with basic daily stress. As we become more stressed, the mind becomes hyperactive and we lose the ability to make clear decisions, think positively, feel enthusiasm, and sleep soundly.

Emotional stress can be triggered by difficulties with a relationship, work environment, or any stress beyond our normal limits. Emotional stress manifests as irritability, anger, lust, depression, and emotional instability. It affects sleep differently from mental stress in that it can cause one to wake up during the night, usually at the pitta time (10 p.m. – 2 a.m.), and leave one unable to go back to sleep. Emotional stress disturbs *sadhaka pitta*, the mind-body conductor responsible for the emotions and functioning of the heart.

As many ways as there are for creating stress there are equally as many possibilities for alleviating it. One should work toward the goals of eliminating the sources of stress and changing one's reactions to stress-provoking situations.

As we can see, it is not just physical toxins that need to be removed. There can also be a buildup of emotional and mental toxins. These toxins get stuck in the cells of the body. This comes from both external and internal stimulus and impressions. These can lead to serious illness and break down of the human body and spirit.

We experience life as stressful due to the pressures of our jobs, family obligations, expectations, never-ending tasks, and deadlines. We sit stagnant a majority of the day without regular and consistent movement. Just as our bodies are burdened by an onslaught of synthetic chemicals and poisons, our minds have become polluted with useless images and excess stimulation. We have detached from nature and its natural biorhythms. Instead of conversations with real people we are often communicating through emojis and abbreviated words. In 2018 it was stated that 93% of death in the world is due to chronic disease and the other 7% natural causes. If we want to be healthy it is essential that we restore balance to our lives. Good health requires communicating with the people around us, our environment, and with Nature in a balanced way. Life is supposed to be a celebration of Love and Consciousness, and it can be if we understand how to rebalance ourselves.

Furthermore, we should live in nature, or as close to it as possible. When we examine modern day society and its conditions of living, the picture is bleak. There is almost no sign of natural living. Instead, we are surrounded by streets, buildings, cars, chemically painted walls, furniture made of synthetic material, clothing made from chemical content, and household cleaning agents that are mostly made of carcinogenic materials. Those who live in big cities and spend most of their lives in human made environments far from nature have an urgent need to create a way to live a more balanced and nature-oriented life. There is an overwhelming need in the modern world for regular detoxification. This can be done on a daily, weekly, monthly, seasonally, or annual schedule.

Mental detoxification can be as simple as taking a day of silence. If you are like most of the modern world and have become dependent on electronic gadgets, unplugging would be a great plan of action, or non-action! Turn off all computers, cell phones, iPads, or any other electronic device you may be habituated to for a day. Spend the day outside in nature. Take deep, long, slow inhalations and exhalations. Stop and smell the roses! Find a clean natural body of water and wash away all worries and stress. Hug the trees and sing to the plants.

When To Do an Internal At-home Cleanse

Over half the population suffers from one symptom or another manifesting as chronic health issues. Sometimes it's small little symptoms such as achy joints or muscles, brain fog, fatigue, headaches, allergies, or gas and bloating. Other times there are more serious problems like autoimmune diseases, migraines, asthma, acne, IBS, acid reflux, arthritis, or worse, cancer.

An internal detoxification may solve these and other problems. An intelligently designed detoxification plan helps you purge more than just unwanted toxins. This is your chance to heal your body on a very deep level. You will find that your energy, sleep, mood, mental clarity, and empathy improve. Those acute or chronic problems will get better or disappear entirely.

While our bodies do have the inherent ability to self-cleanse, they also give us indications when extra help is needed, which is what "symptoms" are. Your lymphatic and immune systems, liver, and kidneys work simultaneously to remove toxins from your body as soon as they enter it. However, if the toxins going in exceed the body's ability to remove them, they get stored inside of our bodies for long periods of time. Just like cleaning the radiator of a car, we must take action to remove these toxins from our bodies.

The 15 Most Common Signs Your
Body Needs Cleansing

1. **You** crave sugar and carbs, especially shortly after eating and between meals.
2. **You** experience digestive distress like gas, bloating, constipation, or diarrhea.

3. You feel spacy or foggy (i.e. "brain fog").

4. You're always tired or exhausted.

5. Your joints and muscles feel achy, painful, or inflamed.

6. You feel stressed, depressed, or anxious on a regular basis.

7. You are overweight and have difficulty losing weight.

8. You have trouble sleeping (falling asleep or sleeping too long).

9. You experience frequent headaches and/or lack of mental clarity.

10. You feel emotionally unstable, unmotivated, and lack energy and enthusiasm for life.

11. You often have skin breakouts and blemishes and/or a dull and lack-luster complexion.

12. You easily catch colds, flues, bugs, and viruses, or have seasonal allergies.

13. You often eat fried foods, dairy, gluten, processed foods, refined or artificial sugar, or fast food.

14. You are exposed to or use common environmental toxins such as carbon emissions, cigarette smoke, herbicides, pesticides, artificial fragrances, and household chemicals.

15. You have bad breath and/or body odor.

The Need to Cleanse the Lymphatic System

The lymphatic system drains the wastes from the body and controls and regulates the immune system. It flows through muscular contractions, so if one is sedentary, the lymphatic system will also eventually become sedentary. This will create toxicity in lymphatic-related tissues such as the breasts, skin, joints, and muscles. Cleansing the body helps detox and nourish the lymphatic system.

Symptoms of sluggish or toxic lymph

- Headaches
- Bloating around the abdomen

- Breast swelling or tenderness
- Cellulite
- Cold hands and feet
- Fatigue and lack of mental clarity
- Itching skin
- Joint discomfort that moves around the body
- Constipation
- Sore or scratchy throat
- Sore feet in the morning
- Swollen hands or feet
- Water retention
- Weakened or low immunity

Benefits of detoxifying the lymphatic system

- Prevention of chronic diseases
- Stronger immunity
- Weight loss
- Improved quality of life
- Increased energy
- Radiant skin
- Bright, clear eyes
- Mental clarity
- Balanced emotions
- Improved self-confidence and empowerment
- New healthy habits and routines
- Improved longevity

The best time for a detoxification program is when you have the capacity to rest. The length of time depends on the necessity to rid the body of toxins. These programs can be done for 5-35 days. During this time, you should go to bed by 9:00 p.m. and have minimal or no social or work commitments. It is important to do a short cleanse and relax on a regular basis. You can do an internal, at-home cleanse up to four times a year. If you typically experience symptoms like coughs, congestion, weakened immunity, or allergies during a particular season, it is good to do a cleanse four to six weeks prior to when you usually experience symptoms. Do not do this cleanse during a fever or menstruation. Doing a yearly cleanse is a traditional part of naturopathy and Ayurveda. Seasonal cleansing was considered an essential factor in creating health and longevity.

2

What is Ayurveda?

Ayurveda is the traditional natural healing system of India. The concept of Ayurveda is not just focused on medical treatment or diagnosis of a diseased condition; it is a set of practical, simple guidelines for living a long and healthful life. Through these principles, we can bring our bodies and minds into perfect balance. Ayurveda has a theoretical basis, but is also completely practical in nature. The word "Ayurveda" is composed of two words—*ayu* and *veda*. *Ayu* means "life," and *veda* means "science." Together, the words mean "the knowledge of life." In Ayurveda, the process of *ayu* is considered a combined experience of body, senses, psyche/mind, and soul. *Ayu* represents all aspects of life, including death, dying, and immortality.

Ayurveda, the "science of life," is the ancient wisdom science of living in harmony with each other and our environment. It is a part of the spiritual tradition of *Sanatana Dharma*, or Universal Truth or Way. Because Sanatana Dharma transcends all caste, nationality, and religion, it is applicable to all people of all places and times. The knowledge of Ayurveda was given to us by the ancient *rishis* (seers). It expounds spiritual insights for living happy, healthy, and peaceful lives, while seeking the ultimate goal of Self-realization. Ayurveda also incorporates the mystical science of Yoga and *Vedanta* (the philosophy of non-dual or unified consciousness). The knowledge of Ayurveda is found in all of the four *Vedas*. The main Ayurvedic text, the *Charaka Samhita*, describes the nature of the universe with all its manifestations, and how to bring our Self into harmony with it. The sayings "We are the microcosm of the macrocosm," and "As above, so below," eloquently explain the universal truth that the whole universe is interconnected and interdependent. Ayurveda declares that real freedom from disease can only be obtained through Self-knowledge. Ayurveda is a path to Self-realization as much as it is a method of managing disease and remaining healthy. Ayurveda aims to manage disease in such a way that it eventually leads the patient to Self-realization.

The science of Ayurveda has developed over thousands of years. Today, it is at the forefront of body-mind-spirit medicines. Ayurveda has expanded far beyond its traditional base in India and is gaining recognition throughout the world. With its profoundly comprehensive understanding of life and consciousness, it is slowly becoming the medicine of the present and future.

Ayurveda says *svasthyatura parayanaha jivitam ayuhu.* This means that the secret of health is not about administering medicine to cause healing, but managing health in such a manner that no disease ever visits. The same thing is said by Hippocrates, the father of modern medicine – "Let food be your medicine and medicine be your food." The main aims of Ayurveda are the prevention, treatment, and cure of disease, as well as the promotion of health on four levels: physical, mental, emotional, and spiritual. Ayurveda teaches us how to create balance in order to attain perfect health. As we better understand the union of our body, mind, and soul, we are able to extend our life span and enhance our well-being.

The deeper purpose of this science, however, is to provide the opportunity for Self-realization, to know the true Self, *sat cit ananda* (Existence-Consciousness-Bliss). We must recognize that our bodies and minds constantly change and that we live in a world of duality. Our task is to discover the veiled part of us that is always there – the knower, the seer, the infinite, unchanging Source. With diligence, perseverance, and patience, we can wake up from *maya* (the dream/illusion) and become free of suffering. As we awaken to our true Self, we create freedom in our body-mind-spirit. Ayurveda recognizes that we came to this earth to remember who we are and to follow that *dharma* (duty), to learn to take care of this physical existence while seeking *moksha* (liberation). When harmony of body, mind, and spirit is established, we become free.

Aspects Unique to Ayurveda

- Ayurveda offers clear direction for managing treatment specific to each individual.
- Ayurvedic theory, with its profound understanding of causal factors in disease manifestation, includes analysis and diagnosis of the individual constitution.
- Ayurveda can be used to structure holistic models of the physical, mental, emotional, and spiritual state of each person, and to create a vision or goal for a balanced state of being.
- Ayurveda offers specific recommendations to each individual on lifestyle, diet, exercise, yoga, herbal therapy, and spiritual practices to restore and maintain balance in body and mind.

3

Overview of 5-35 Day Ayurvedic Home Cleanse

Daily Regimen (Dinacharya)

- Wake Up – Ideally an hour or more before sunrise, the best time for meditation and yoga
- Oral Hygiene – Brush teeth, scrape tongue, *gandusha* (oil pulling)
- Abhyanga – Self-oilation/massage
- Nasya – Administer medicated nasal drops in the morning and early to mid-afternoon
- Meditation – Twice a day, in the morning and again before bed
- Pranayama – Mindful breathing
- Exercise – Surya Namaskar (Sun salutation yoga sequence), Qi Kung, Tai Chi, walking, etc.
- Shodhana (Purification) – *basti* (enema) and *swedhana* (sweating)
- Rest – It is essential to keep all work/social responsibilities to an absolute minimum, if any at all, and avoid physical exertion
- Pratyahara (Sensory Withdrawal) – Avoid external stimuli like screens (computer, cell phone, iPad, etc.), social media, television
- Sleep – Before 9:00 p.m., sleep 7-8 hours
- Before Bed:
- Bath – Take a warm (not too hot!) bath with Epsom salt and lavender essential oil

- Abhyanga – Apply oil to the head, hands and feet; massage each area for 3-5 minutes

Ahara (Food/Diet Therapy)

Hydration

Drink sufficient quantity of pure water every day. Start the day with 500-750 ml of warm water. For a deeper detoxification the water can be boiled with ginger and lemon added. Start the day with hot lemon ginger water.

Diet

- 2-3 specialized meals per day (No snacking!)
- Eat organic seasonal vegetables and kichari.
- Eat a light breakfast, a medium to large sized lunch, and a light and early dinner.
- Sip hot water every 10-15 minutes throughout the day.
- If possible and suitable for your constitution, skip dinner.

Purification Supplements

Digestive Detox Tea: 1 cup in the morning and evening

Triphala: 3 g (capsule or powder) 1-2 hours after dinner with a teaspoon of ghee or honey or a cup of warm water or digestive detox tea

Turmeric: 1-2 g after each meal

Activated Charcoal: Take 1 g in the evening 1-2 hours after dinner

Digestive Enzymes: Use a comprehensive digestive enzyme before each meal

Candida: If you know you have an overgrowth of *Candida albicans*, there are numerous enzyme and herbal based formulas designed to kill and remove the overgrowth. It is recommended to find one suitable for you to take during the cleanse.

Probiotics: Take after completing the cleanse to recolonize friendly flora

Shodhana (Flushing Out the dosha)

Basti (Enemas): Performing a daily enema will assist in removing toxins from the g.i. tract..

Swedhana (Sweating): Daily or every other day depending on the type of sweating. Depending on body type one can do steam, dry, or far infrared sauna.

Completing the Cleanse and Reintegrating

After cleansing, it is critical to repopulate the gut with friendly bacteria in order to grow a healthy microbiome. There are several ways to do this:

Triphala – Triphala is a good to continue long term, even if your bowel/elimination is balanced. It is *tridoshic* and supports ongoing health and vitality.

Turmeric – 1 g after each meal.

Probiotics – To be taken after the cleanse is complete in order to recolonize friendly flora.

Dinacharya – These practices should be practiced one's whole lifespan. They protect the body against toxic build up and pathogenic invaders.

Diet – Determine your *dosha* (bodily constitution) and maintain a diet suitable for you. Staying hydrated and avoiding snacks is key in keeping metabolic waste out of the body.

4

Dinacharya (Daily Regime)

Dinacharya means to follow the cycles of the day. It also means to live in harmony with the rhythms of Mother Nature. Living in accordance with nature and nature's circadian rhythms balances our inner ecology. This state of balance assists us in adjusting and flowing with the ever-changing environment. Being in tune with nature and her rhythm attunes us to our own human nature and Divine Self. This state of balance is where we attain perfect health. The *rishis* considered daily routine to be a stronger healing force than any other curative medicine. Today, society is out of touch with nature. For example, on any given day, very few people know where the moon is in its cycle. In order for us to really heal, we must re-attune ourselves to nature's cycles.

Waking & Sleeping with the Natural Cycles

Din means "day," and *acharya* means "to follow, to find, close to." To follow or be close to the day implies unifying your daily routine with the natural cycle of the sun, moon, earth, and the other planets. Following dinacharya is one of the best means to align with nature. This creates balance and prevents disease. Ultimately, we will find that health and happiness are one's natural state.

Brahma Mahurta (The Divine Time) 2-6 a.m. It is not recommended that everyone should wake up at 2 a.m. It is encouraged during the cleansing to rest completely (i.e. 7-8 hours). If you go to sleep by 9 p.m., waking up between 4 and 5 a.m. is perfect. This is one to two hours before sunrise.

It is natural to wake up to go to the toilet at this time because our bodily systems are awake if we sleep during the proper hour. If you get up naturally to go to the toilet, stay awake and do your morning program. *Vata* or *prana dosha* (air and space element) governs this time, which influences the environment with serene, calm, creative, and clear energy. This time of day is the most *sattvic* (pure) and is best for meditation and yoga. Waking up with this energy and these qualities allows them to stay with you for the rest of the day. If you are in the habit of waking up after sunrise, get up without hitting the snooze button and proceed with the morning program. Be in bed before 9 p.m. when the earth element (*kapha*) is governing. This is perfect time for deep rest and rejuvenation.

Oral Hygiene

Brushing Teeth and Scraping Tongue
Brushing the teeth and scraping the tongue is the first part of the morning cleansing regime. If you have whitish or yellowish coating on your tongue when you wake up every morning, it means toxins are being expelled from the body. This is accumulated toxic residue from the day before. Gently scrape it off with a stainless steel tongue scraper within the first 3 minutes of waking. This will assure that the toxins are not reabsorbed back into your body. Nine passes over the tongue from back to front should remove the previous days toxic build up. Do more if necessary.

Gandusha (Oil Pulling)
Gandusha or oil pulling is the process of swishing 1 tsp to 1 tbsp of oil (cold-pressed sesame or coconut oil) in the mouth for 15-20 minutes. It is an ancient practice to remove bacteria, which removes

bad breath, and promote oral hygiene. It reduces inflammation in the gums, prevents cavities, and strengthens the teeth and gums.

Oil pulling is easy to do because you can do it simultaneously with almost anything. It can be done during self-massage, yoga, meditation, in the shower, or making tea. This can be in the morning after scraping the tongue and again after brushing the teeth before bed. After you spit the oil out, rinse your mouth with warm water.

Abhyanga (Application of Oil)

Abhyanga is the external application of therapeutic and rejuvenating natural oils. It soothes, softens, and lubricates the bodily tissues so that toxins are easily released. The skin is an organ of assimilation and elimination. Abhyanga is highly useful in maintaining immunity, nourishing various tissues of the body, and cleansing impurities. It improves lymphatic and cardiac circulation and is also helpful for stiffness, fatigue, constipation, dry skin, diseases of the nervous system, tremors, and osteoarthritis. Abyhanga relaxes the mind and promotes inner tranquility. When done regularly, abhyanga creates lasting feelings of calm acceptance and gratitude.

Many people apply moisturizer daily. Ayurveda encourages you to replace that moisturizer with oil. Sesame or coconut is good but a medicated oil like Brahmi thailam, Dashamoola thailam or Ashwagnadha thailam is preferred. Apply the oil, give yourself a gentle massage, and let it absorb into the body for 30 minutes or more. Then take a warm bath or shower. Do not wash the oil off with soap. Use a loofah sponge or organic cotton wash cloth. During the cleansing process and after it is recommended to do abhyanga daily. If you are inspired, morning or evening is great.

Exercise

*There is nothing to equal the supreme joy felt by
the Yogi of pure mind who has attained the state
of pure consciousness and overcome death.*

~ Yoga Vasistha Sara, verse 4.25

Hatha Yoga (yoga *asanas*) is important for dissolving physical tension and calming the mind before meditation. It is the perfect ayurvedic exercise because it rejuvenates the body, improves digestion, and removes stress. It can be done by anyone of any age. Yoga asanas (postures) can balance all three doshas. Yoga tonifies every area of the body and cleanses the internal organs of toxins, which is one of the primary goals of Ayurveda.

Surya Namaskar (Sun Salutation)

For centuries, we have bowed and offered prayers to the Sun, the source of life on Earth. It is believed that an element of the Sun is present in everything we eat, drink, and breathe.

Surya Namaskar is an ancient discipline of expressing gratitude towards the source of life, the Sun, through the practice of 12 different postures. The 12 asanas of the Sun Salutation are designed to synchronize the physical and inner *prana* cycles with the external solar cycles. This synchronicity helps to maintain a level of vibrancy, radiance, and receptivity, helping one to manifest a body and spirit that is fit to be absorbed in higher consciousness. It is a complete workout for the physical and subtle bodies and for awakening our inner light.

Surya Namaskar is the most complete yoga vinyasa (flow sequence) available as it provides balance, strength, and flexibility to all major muscles in the body. It supports the flow of prana throughout the whole body. Surya Namaskar can be done once or twice a day; at sunrise, sunset, after *abhyanga* and before showering, or whenever you want, with the exception of before bed. Surya

Namaskar done in a traditional way, as prescribed by yogic texts, should be performed at the time of sunrise, facing the sun, and letting its rays fall freely on the body. Do the sequences according to your ability and comfort. You should not strain. This practice should be relaxed and joyful. After Surya Namaskar is complete, lie down in *Savasana* (Corpse Pose) for 5-10 minutes without falling asleep. Pay attention to your breath.

Surya Namaskar is a complete yogic exercise. It blesses the body by giving the benefit of all asanas while incorporating natural *pranayama*. It can be done in cycles from 6 to 108 depending upon the physical fitness level of the individual.

Traditionally, there are 12 poses involved in one Surya Namaskar, and every pose will be accompanied by chanting each of the 12 names of the Sun god. Doing Surya Namaskar in a traditional way may not be possible for many due to various practical difficulties. Such persons may do them at any convenient time on an empty stomach. In this case, they do not need to chant the 12 names of the Sun god. The mantras *Ma* (symbolizing divine love) and *Om* (symbolizing divine light) can be silently infused with the ingoing and outgoing breath. *Ma* belongs to the *Puraka* (inhalation), and *Om* belongs to the *Rechaka* (exhalation).

Gently do 6-12 Surya Namaskars (1 repetition = the sequence completed on both sides of the body).

Basic Surya Namaskar Mantra and Instruction

Position 1
Om Mitraya Namaha
(Prostrations to Him who is affectionate to all.)
Start in a standing position, facing the sun. Both your feet should touch each other, palms joined together in prayer pose.

Position 2
Om Ravaye Namaha

(Prostrations to Him who is the cause of change.)
With a deep inhalation, raise both arms above your head and tilt slightly backward, arching your back.

Position 3
Om Suryaya Namaha
(Prostrations to Him who induces activity.)
With a deep exhalation, bend forward and touch the mat, both palms in line with your feet, forehead touching your knees.

Position 4
Om Bhanave Namaha
(Prostrations to Him who diffuses light.)
With a deep inhalation, take your right leg away from your body in a big, backward step. Both your hands should be firmly planted on your mat, your left foot between your hands, head tilted towards the ceiling.

Position 5
Om Khagaya Namaha
(Prostrations to Him who moves in the sky.)
With a deep inhalation, take your left leg away from your body in a big, backward step. Both your hands should be firmly planted on your mat, head tilted toward the ceiling.

Position 6
Om Pushne Namaha
(Prostrations to Him who nourishes all.)
With a deep exhalation, shove your hips and butt up toward the ceiling, forming an upward arch. Your arms should be straight and aligned with your head.

Position 7
Om Hiranyagarbhaya Namaha
(Prostrations to Him who contains all wealth.)
With a deep exhalation, lower your body down until your forehead, chest, knees, hands and feet are touching the mat, your butt tilted up. Take a normal breath in this pose.

Position 8
Om Marichaye Namaha
(Prostrations to Him who possesses rays.)
With a deep inhalation, slowly snake forward till your head is up, your back arched and concave as much as possible.

Position 9
Om Adityaya Namaha
(Prostrations to Him who is the Son of Aditi.)
Exhaling deeply, again push your butt and hips up toward the ceiling as in position six, arms aligned straight with your head.

Position 10
Om Savitre Namaha
(Prostration to Him who is fit to be worshipped.)

Inhaling deeply, bring your right foot in toward your body in a big, forward step. Both your hands should be planted firmly on your mat, right foot between your hands, head tilted toward the ceiling.

Position 11
Om Arkaya Namaha
(Prostrations to Him who is the reproducer of everything.)
Exhaling deeply, bring your left foot in toward your body, rise up and touch the mat, keeping both your palms in line with your feet, forehead touching your knees.

Position 12
Om Bhaskaraya Namaha
(Prostrations to Him who is the cause of luster.)
Inhaling deeply, raise both your arms above your head and tilt slightly backward.
Return to stand facing the sun, both feet touching, palms joined together in prayer pose.

Practical Benefits of Surya Namaskar

• Surya Namaskar strengthens the heart, improves circulation, digestive fire, and awakens and revitalizes the mind.
• Surya Namaskar is a workout for the muscles, joints, ligaments, and skeletal system.
• Surya Namaskar improves posture and balance. The limbs become symmetrical while the internal vital organs are massaged and become more functional.
• Surya Namaskar is beneficial for a healthy digestive system. Blood flow is increased to the digestive tract, stimulating peristalsis so that digestion is more efficient. Yoga is calming, which relaxes the digestive system and leads to more effective and efficient elimination.
• Surya Namaskar eases insomnia and other sleep-related disorders as it calms the mind.

- Surya Namaskar practice regulates hormones and irregular menstrual cycles.
- Surya Namaskar increases blood circulation.
- Surya Namaskar helps to burn calories and stay fit. Practicing Surya Namaskar is one of the easiest ways to stay in shape. Because it stretches the abdominal muscles, regular practice helps to lose excessive belly fat and gives a flat stomach.
- Surya Namaskar stimulate sluggish glands to increase their hormonal secretions. The thyroid gland especially has a huge effect on weight balance as it affects body metabolism.
- Surya Namaskar adds a glow to the face, making facial skin radiant and ageless. It is a natural solution to prevent the onset of wrinkles. Overall, yoga is excellent for the skin.
- Surya Namaskar boosts one's natural endurance. It promotes ojas (vitality and strength). It also reduces the feelings of restlessness and anxiety.
- Surya Namaskar makes the whole body more flexible, especially the spine and limbs.
- Surya Namaskar regulates the pineal gland and hypothalamus to prevent pineal degeneration and calcification. It opens the 72,000 nadis, which are the body's yogic energy meridians.

Walking

It is very important to get fresh air by going outside and being with the Earth. Go for a slow to medium paced relaxed walk in nature each day for 30-60 minutes. If you are too toxic and too sick to do this, at least go outside in the grass or near a tree and sit for some time and do deep relaxed belly breathing. Walking is a universal exercise that is suitable for people of all ages.

Other Exercises

Beyond yoga and walking, swimming, cycling, and jogging are excellent exercises that can be practiced alone or in conjunction with a daily yoga practice. Skipping is an exercise, which can be done with a great health advantage to keep fit and energetic. Skipping is one of the cheapest, most effective fat-burning workouts you can do, and it does not require much space; it's fun too. It can be done outside in nature as well as in the home in a well-ventilated room. It is a superb exercise for the heart, lungs and blood circulation. If it is done properly, it can give the same benefit of one hour of walking or half an hour of jogging in as little time as only five minutes. However, people with poor lungs, a weak heart, or arthritis should first consult an expert before skipping. Among all the forms of exercises, yoga asanas are the best as they can beautifully harmonize the flow of prana to all the body parts as no other exercises can. They take care of all the vital organs, nerves, spine, and the brain. Apart from this, they bring peace to the mind and calmness to the subconscious mind, hence they are considered spiritual exercises.

Nasya – Nasal Drops

Nasya is the nasal administration of medicinal herbs, decoctions, and oils. Different types of substances are used to treat many various ailments. Nasya oil can be an herbal infused medicated oil or a plain oil like sesame or coconut, which is both nurturing and nourishing, and supports the sinus, nose, throat, and head. It is a balancing formula for all *dosha* types and supports the proper flow of *prana*. Nasya has been traditionally used to lubricate the nasal passages, improve the voice, and support clear vision. Prana, the vital life force, enters our bodies through the breath. Lubrication of the nasal passages with herbal oil provides subtle moisture to the air we breathe and affects the higher cerebral faculties and sensory organs. It promotes clarity of perception and stimulates memory. Regular application of nasya oil enhances cerebral circulation, restoring and balancing prana in the body.

The nose is the door to consciousness, mind, and brain as well as the pathway to our inner pharmacy. This inner pharmacy is governed by the pineal and pituitary glands. The quickest route to the pineal and pituitary gland is via the nasal passage. Medications that are administered via the nasal passages affect the mind and nervous system in profound ways. Herbal nasya oil lubricates, protects and calms the mind. Applying nasya oil lubricates the nasal passage and treats most imbalances related to ear, neck, throat and head. It helps in preventing allergies, headaches, earaches and sore throats. It is amazing in its ability to relieve tension from the neck, head and shoulder area. It also gives incredible focus and mental clarity.

Instructions:

Lie flat on your back with your head tilted so the oil can naturally flow down through your nostrils. Apply 3-5 drops of nasya oil or sesame oil in left nostril and inhale deeply 3x through the nose and out through the mouth. Repeat this in the right nostril. Then lie there breathing naturally for five minutes. Sniffing the oil brings it to the brain, which stimulates the glymphatic system (brain/lymph system) to decalcify the pineal gland, detox emotions, pacify stress, regulate hormones, and strengthen and improve the sensory organs. This also helps to regulate the flow of prana through the 72,000 *nadis* (subtle nerve channels) of the body. If you get the oil in your throat and feel discomfort, breathe slowly with awareness. This will soon pass and you will get used to it. After sitting up you can spit out any oil accumulated in the throat and sip some warm water.

If this method is too intense, it can be done while seated. Place a drop of nasya oil on the little finger and gently insert it into a nostril. Gently massage the inner walls of the nasal passage for a minute or two. Alternate left and right nostrils until each nostril has received a total of three applications of oil.

Meditation

I only went out for a walk and finally concluded to stay out till sundown, for going out, I found, was really going in.

~ John Muir

Meditation is the saving principle; it makes you immortal and eternal. Meditation takes you across the cycle of death and rebirth. Meditation is ambrosia. It actually prevents the fear of death. It makes you egoless and takes you to the state of no-mind. Once you transcend the mind, you cannot die. Meditation and spiritual practices give you the power and courage to smile at death. Meditation helps you see everything as a delightful play so that even the moment of death becomes a blissful experience.

~ Amma (Awaken Children Vol. 8, pg. 135-137)

The power of true meditation is unfathomable. Real meditation is simply the mind's natural state of awareness or being. Meditation is the greatest way of keeping the mind still and clear. It promotes an optimistic outlook on life, and a cheerful attitude and positive thinking promote strong mental health as well as physical well-being. The physical benefits of meditation are now being documented and utilized by the Western medical system. Meditation helps to normalize blood pressure, pulse rate, and levels of stress hormones in the blood. It produces changes to the neuro-hormones in the brain, creating a calming, nourishing effect. Meditation can raise pain-bearing capacity, eliminating dependency on painkillers that create adverse side effects.

Meditation allows one to realize that they are not the temporal, physical body subject to change from birth, growth, old age, disease and, inevitably, death. Meditation also helps one realize that one is not the mind that constantly fluctuates from one thought or emotion to another, like happiness, sorrow, boredom, anger, jealousy, and so on. True meditation brings us to the state of awareness that we are the *Paramatman* (The Supreme Consciousness), whose very nature is bliss that is absolute, infinite, and changeless. In this state of awareness, all the disturbances pertaining to the body and mind are instantly reduced to nothingness, just as burnt camphor leaves no trace. True meditation involves relaxing all the muscles, releasing all worldly thoughts, and thinking one-pointedly about any aspect of divinity, God, or a *Satguru* (perfect master). The unmatched benefit of meditation is that it purifies the body, mind, and *chitta* (subconscious mind). Meditation gives the body radiant health and the mind clarity. Meditation liberates us and transforms our whole life and consciousness from the human level to a divine level.

Daily meditation, for approximately 20-30 minutes, allows us the time and space to tune in to our Higher Selves and discover the space of Love in our hearts and consciousness. The goal and intention of all forms of meditation is to create an internal state of mental peace and contentment. This is the best way to start and end the day. While it ultimately doesn't matter which meditation technique you choose, I recommend learning and doing a meditation technique given by a Perfect Master.

Amma has given us several meditation techniques that can be performed daily. Amma Herself has created the "White Flowers of Peace" meditation. Amma says, "When practiced by many, whether together or apart, as each one lights their own candle, let the darkness of ignorance be dispelled forever; may peace and happiness prevail." This guided meditation is available digitally through www.theammashop.org. Another meditation practice given by Amma is the *Ma-Om* meditation that infuses the vibrations of *Ma* (Divine Unconditional Love) and *Om* (Universal Light) with the breath. The audio of Amma guiding this practice is also available via the online Amma shop.

In 2003, Amma created IAM – Integrated Amrita Meditation Technique®. The meditation technique introduced here is called 'Integrated Amrita Meditation Technique®' because its goal is the integration of body, breath, and mind. It is a combination of relaxing yogic stretches, breathing and concentration exercises and takes only 35 minutes a day. IAM is a suitable practice for almost anyone and is not bound to any religious or spiritual belief system. This practice is taught worldwide in numerous languages. For more information visit: www.iam-meditation.org/the-meditation-technique/

"The remote control of our mind should rest firmly in the palm of our hand." Imagine one with such mental control. Emotions, ideas, and memories are at his beck and call. If anger comes, he can change the channel. The same with jealousy and greed. He can recall any past event, like reversing a DVD. If he wants ideas, he only need turn to the "idea channel" and a stream of creative ideas will flow forth. No more staring at the blank screen of writer's block. Total and complete mental control—this is what IAM (Meditation) offers."

~ Amma

Meditation is a truly worthwhile activity that can be done anywhere and anytime. It will put you in direct touch with the never-ending source of joy and happiness.

Amma says, "Children, you should live with the remembrance of God. Your heart should constantly throb for God. There shouldn't be a single instant when you do not remember God. Constant thought directed to God is meditation, like the flow of a river. Do not waste time. Repeat your mantra while doing every action. Every day, meditate for some time."

Mantra As Meditation

In the beginning was the Word. And the Word was with God and the Word was God.

~ The Bible

In the present dark age of materialism, the constant repetition of a mantra is the easiest way to obtain inner purification and concentration. You can chant your mantra at anytime, anywhere, without observing any rules regarding purity of body or mind. It can be done while engaged in any task. Mental purity will come through constant chanting of the

*divine name. This is the simplest way. You are trying to cross
the ocean of transmigration, the cycle of birth and death. The
mantra is the oar of the boat; it is the instrument you use
to cross the samsara of your restless mind, with its unending
thought waves. The mantra can also be compared to a ladder
that you climb to reach the heights of God-realization.*

~ Amma

What is a Mantra?

Om Mantra-Sarayai Namah
I bow to She who is the essence of all mantras.
~ Sri Lalita Sahasranama, Verse 846

Mantras intone sound in the purest and most original form. *Mantra
japa* (repetition of a mantra) is extraordinarily powerful because it
connects us with the original divine energy. When we connect to
divine energy, we are relieved of suffering. This is why the Sanskrit
meaning of mantra is, "saving the mind from suffering and illness."

According to Ayurveda, mantras invoke the divine energy to
flow into us. The way this happens is quite simple. All sentient and
non-sentient forms in the universe are composed of different energies, and all the energies in the universe have an associated sound
vibration. Modern physics confirms this: All forms in the universe
are composed of energy-emitting vibrations. It follows logically that
when we chant sounds associated with divine energy, we too begin
to vibrate at the same frequency as the Divine.

Historically, Buddhism and Hinduism have used mantras for
spiritual growth and healing. For example, in the shamanic traditions of Tibetan Ayurveda, there is a detailed system of healing that
uses mantras for the treatment of numerous diseases. In ancient
India, mastering the chanting of mantras was part of Ayurvedic
training. Only one who mastered the science of mantras could be
called an *Ayurveda Acharya* (one proficient in Ayurveda). Vedic texts

declare, "By reciting mantras, one can conquer decay, aversion, loss of appetite (dyspepsia), leprosy, disorders of the stomach, cough, asthma, etc. The doer of mantra earns great merit, and in his [or her] next birth attains salvation, which is the portion of the noblest beings." Thus, everything from health and wealth to liberation can be attained by mantra japa.

Historically, mantras were verbally transmitted from master to student when the student was ready. Amma, one of the greatest living masters, generally offers mantras to those who express interest, while emphasizing that one must be ready to put forth effort once receiving the mantra. She describes the process: "Children, when Amma gives you a mantra, she sows a seed of spirituality within you. She transmits a part of herself into your heart. But, you have to work on it. You have to nurture that seed by meditating, praying and chanting your mantra regularly, without fail. You have to be totally committed." If we commit to chanting our mantra, our entire life will change for the better. Amma explains that, "By chanting your mantra, your entire being will be transformed and you will realize your divine nature."

If you have not yet come into contact with a Perfect Master (*Satguru*) who can transmit a mantra to you directly, you can chose from numerous mantras that can be chanted safely with powerful results. They are profoundly effective for all human beings, regardless of one's cultural heritage, spiritual/religious background, age, or gender.

In order to achieve our physical, emotional, mental, and spiritual goals, it is vitally important that we practice mantra japa regularly. Effort is required for any undertaking to be successful, and the path of Self-realization is no different. As we put loving effort into our mantra japa practice, grace will flow into us. As more grace comes our way, we find the strength to put forth more effort. Amma says, "The period of sadhana is like climbing a high mountain. You need a lot of strength and energy. Mountain climbers use a rope to pull themselves up. For you, the only rope is japa. Therefore, children, try to repeat your mantra constantly. Once you reach the peak, you can relax and rest forever."

Thus, we should attempt to chant our mantra constantly. Fortunately, there are no rules about purity when doing mantra japa. Mantras can be chanted anywhere, anytime. While bathing, cooking, eating, driving, walking, exercising, or shopping, mantra japa can ceaselessly flow, either out loud or silently in the mind.

It is important to understand that while chanting, one should attempt to practice mantra japa with the proper attitude. This is because the effectiveness of a mantra depends upon the mental and emotional disposition of the person repeating it. Just like the saying, "Sweetness depends upon the amount of sugar put in," the greater the faith and devotion, the greater the power of the mantra. When we chant with the proper inner disposition, our practice will blossom. The physical vibration unified with the right mental intention, increases the influence of the mantra. Hence the great metaphysical saying, "Energy flows where intention goes."

Amma suggests, "Do japa (mantra repetition) with alertness. Each repetition should be like savoring a sweet. In the end, you will reach a state where even if you let go of the mantra, the mantra won't let go of you." For this reason, it is very beneficial to set aside some time each day to sit and repeat mantras and then meditate quietly for some time to feel the vibrations reverberating inside your being.

While mantras can and should be chanted anywhere and anytime, there are specific places that are considered the most conducive for gaining concentration. Any place where an enlightened being has been is sanctified and is therefore an ideal place for chanting. The Vedas mention the following natural environments as the best for meditation and mantra japa:

1. Flower gardens

2. Natural places of solitude, i.e., rivers, mountains, lakes, caves, etc.

3. In the middle of a forest

4. Any place where no war has occurred

5. **Any** holy place or place of pilgrimage
6. **Mountain** caves
7. **Underneath** a banyan, bilva, or peepal tree
8. **Next** to a tulasi plant
9. **On** the banks of a river
10. **Near** a pond or a spring (fresh water)

Other places conducive for concentrated chanting are near cows, streams, a ghee lamp, or a temple. It is also best to chant in early morning or late afternoon sun, under the full moon, or in the presence of a Perfect Master. It is also said that doing mantra japa while sitting in a river or stream so the water is up to the navel or the chest is very purifying. Chanting on the seashore is very *sattvic* and peaceful too, and we also get the healing benefits of the negative ions coming from the ocean.

There are many mantras that can be chanted to balance the body, the five elements, and the *chakras*—and for spiritual growth, peace, and happiness. There are also mantras for the planets. However, it is recommended that a *jyotisha* is consulted before beginning such practices, to ensure proper usage.

Until the point where it is possible to receive a personal mantra from a Perfect Master, like Amma, here are some divine mantras that can be chanted on a regular basis. Their meanings are included:

Om: Om is the primordial sound, the original manifestation of consciousness. It precedes creation and lasts beyond the final dissolution. It is the sound that connects and contains all living beings. Om can be chanted by itself, and is also used at the beginning of any mantra to give it more *shakti* (spiritual power).

Ma: Ma represents the Divine Mother, and also can be repeated by itself. *Ma* embodies the sound of divine Love, the Mother of Creation.

Jai Ma: "Victory to the Divine Mother" or "Praise the Goddess of the Universe."

Om Namah Shivaya: This mantra is one of many ways of praising Lord Shiva. It means, "I bow to the Divine Consciousness."

Om Shivashaktyaikya Rupinyai Namah: "I bow to Her who is the union of Shiva and Shakti in one form." This mantra is for the union of Shiva and Shakti, or *purusha* and *prakriti*. Divine Consciousness and Divine Energy work together to create and sustain the world.

Om Sri Mata Amritanandamayi Devyai Namah: This is a mantra for Amma that means, "I bow to Amma, the Goddess of Immortal Bliss."

Om Amritesvaryai Namah: Another mantra for Amma, it means, "I bow to the Goddess of Immortality."

Om Parashaktyai Namah: "Salutations to the Goddess who is the Supreme Energy." This mantra is for the Goddess of Creation, the supreme energy.

Om Gam Ganapatayai Namah: "Salutations to Lord Ganapati." Ganapati is another name for Ganesha, the remover of all obstacles and the son of Shiva and Parvati.

Om Gam Ganeshaya Namah: "Salutations to Lord Ganesha," another mantra for Ganesha that helps to remove obstacles and bestow grace.

Om Sri Hanumate Namah: "Salutations to the Blessed Lord Hanuman, servant of Lord Rama." This mantra invokes the grace of Hanuman, Son of the Wind, who is endowed with prana. He bestows strength, devotion, and faith.

Om Sri Maha Lakshmyai Namah: "Salutations to the Great Goddess Lakshmi." This mantra is for the Goddess Lakshmi, the goddess of all the wealth, beauty and all types of prosperity in the world.

Om Namo Bhagavate Vasudevaya: "Salutations to the Supreme Lord Vasudeva." Vasudeva is a name of Lord Vishnu, the sustainer of all life in the world. Chanting this protects a devotee from many troubles, and bestows the devotee with peace and prosperity.

Om Mani Padme Hum: A Buddhist mantra meaning, "Salutations to the Jewel of Consciousness [the mind], which resides at the heart's lotus."

Om Tare Tu Tare Ture Svaha: "Salutations to the Supreme Goddess Tara." A mantra to the Buddhist Goddess Tara, an aspect of Kali. She bestows grace and compassion.

Om Ah Hum Vajra Guru Padma Siddhi Hum: "I invoke Vajra Guru, Padmasambhava. May your blessings grant Supreme Realization." The mantra of Padmasambhava evokes blessings that help to overcome all obstacles. Padmasambhava was a historical Tibetan Buddhist Master who is said to have been born in a lotus flower. He was a renowned scholar, meditator, healer, and guru.

Hare Rama Hare Rama, Rama Rama Hare Hare, Hare Krishna Hare Krishna, Krishna Krishna Hare Hare: The Mahamantra, this mantra is for Lord Vishnu, the preserver, in the forms of Rama and Krishna.

Mahamritunjaya Mantra: Om Tryambakam Yajamahe Sugandhim Pushtivardhanam Urvarukam Iva Bandhanan Mrityor Mukshiya Mamritat: "We worship the Three-Eyed One, Shiva, who is divinely fragrant and who nourishes all beings. May he liberate us from death for the sake of immortality, just as a cucumber is severed from the bondage of a creeper." *Mritu* means "death" and *jaya* is "victory." Thus, the mantra verily means, "to grant victory over both the ego and death." This powerful mantra can be chanted to attain good health and release from bondage and to solve many other problems. It has been called the greatest reliever from all evils and can be recited at any time like any other *mahamantra* (great mantra).

Gayatri Mantra: Om Bhur Bhuva Svaha, Tat Savitur Varenyam, Bhargo Devasya Dhimahi, Dhi Yo Yonah Prachodayat: The *Gayatri Mantra* is the universal prayer extolled in the Vedas. It is one of the most commonly chanted mantras. It translates to: *Om* – we meditate (*dhimahi*) upon the spiritual effulgence (*bhargo*) of that adorable supreme divine reality (*varenyam devasya*), the source (*savitur*) of the physical (*bhur*), the astral (*bhuva*), and the heavenly (*svaha*) spheres of existence. May That (*Tat*) supreme divine being enlighten (*prachodayat*) our (*nah*) intellect (*dhiyo*) (so that we may realize the

Supreme Truth). "We meditate upon the Spiritual Effulgence of that Adorable, Supreme, Divine Reality. Please grant us liberation."

Pranayama

Prana is made of two words *pra* (to fill) is added to the root word *an* (to breathe or to live) creating the new meaning "life that fills with breath." *Pranayama* is control of breath. "Prana" is breath or universal life force. On subtle levels, prana represents the pranic energy responsible for life, and *ayama* means control. Therefore, pranayama is "control of breath." One can control the rhythms of prana with pranayama and achieve a healthy body and mind.

From the yoga perspective, pranayama is a series of exercises, which aims at bringing more oxygen to blood and to the brain. It not only automates flow of blood but also regulates proper functioning of thoughts and desire. Control of the breath gives control of the mind and its thoughts. This gives mental strength and tremendous will power. It generates lots of courage and will power within an individual. Pranayama is the practice of controlling our "life-force," or prana. In Hatha Yoga, pranayama includes specific breathing exercises that assist in maintaining the health of the body and achieving deep inner-awareness through stilling the mind. Pranayama leads to inner peace, tranquility, steadiness of mind and good health. A simple form of pranayama is the repetition of mantras along with the inhalation and exhalation. For example, one can practice Amma's *Ma-Om* meditation technique, silently repeating *Ma* while breathing in and *Om* while breathing out and focusing on the vibration of the sound. As we repeat this type of pranayama, the breath and the sound vibration unite as one to take the yogi into deep states of meditation. With movement, the breath of the yogi unifies with the universe and still, conscious, pure awareness awakens.

Anuloma Viloma

This pranayama awakens energy in the body and mind and releases stress and anxiety. It helps to re-establish the gut-brain connection. It supports the production of serotonin, dopamine, melatonin, and other important neuro-hormones. It should be practiced in the morning in fresh air with an empty stomach.

Instructions

- Sit comfortably with the spine straight.
- Close the right nostril with the right thumb and inhale slowly and fully through the left nostril.
- Close the left nostril with the middle and ring finger and exhale completely through the right nostril.
- With the left nostril still closed breathe in slowly and deeply through the right nostril.
- Close the right nostril and breathe out fully through the left nostril.
- Do this repetition for 10-20 minutes.
- Inhalations and exhalation should be equal and full to one's capacity without strain.

Bhramari (Bee Humming)

Bhramari is excellent for releasing agitation, frustration, and anger. It is the best breathing exercise for calming your mind. It alleviates headaches and neck tension. It also alleviates high blood pressure and is beneficial for those with any type of heart disease.

Instructions

- Sit comfortably with the spine erect.
- Place your index fingers on the forehead, close the ears with the thumbs and with the remaining fingers gently lay them across your closed eyes.
- Start inhaling through both nostrils deeply and slowly into the belly.

- While keeping the mouth closed, exhale by making a humming sound like "hmmmm." Focus on the crown of the head and imagine it filling with golden light like honey (Amrita), like a bumble bee making honey, saturating your head with Universal Love or Consciousness.
- Repeat this 7, 11, or 21 times.

Omkara Japa (Chanting the mantra Om)

Omkara mantra should be done after doing *Anuloma Viloma* and *Brahmari pranayama*. This is the sound of creation, the sound of the universe and the highest vibrational frequency!

Instructions

- Breathe fully into the belly, torso, and upper respiratory tract. On the exhalation, loudly express the sound OM. The exhalation should be as long as possible without needing to gasp for the next breath. This can be repeated 3-108 times.
- After finishing Omkara Japa, sit in silent still awareness for as long as possible feeling the vibrations of Unconditional Love and Universal Light.

Bedtime, Bath, And Massage

Start your evening routine 1–1½ hours before going to bed. To wind down and prepare for deep rejuvenating sleep, take a warm bath with Epsom salt and lavender essential oil. It is best to take your bath without bright lights on. You can use a natural candle (beeswax or soy), Himalayan salt lamp, quartz crystal lamp, or natural oil lamp with ghee or sesame oil and a cotton wick.

Spend at least 20 minutes soaking in the bath. During this time you can do the *Ma-Om* or White Flowers of Peace meditation, or simply focus on being in the present moment and allow the concerns of your mind to subside. After drying off, apply a few drops of *Abhyanga* oil to your fingers and rub the oil onto the crown of your head. Then massage both feet with the oil. You may wear natural fiber socks if you want to avoid getting oil on your sheets. Go to sleep before 9 p.m.

Rest

This is the most critical part of the cleanse. You must relax your mind and thoughts as well as your body. Keep work/social responsibilities to an absolute minimum. If possible, avoid all external stimuli such as electronics (computer, phone, iPad, Kindle), social media, and television. This also means verbal stimuli. As much as possible keep talking to a minimum.

Pratyahara, the withdrawing of our senses, allows one to have a true experience of Self. This will allow the cleansing process to go much deeper in rebalancing the psycho-neuro-immunology (*Prana-Tejas-Ojas*). During pratyahara one withdraws the senses from their objects of attachment, shifting one's awareness from external objects to the internal. When our sense faculties become detached from "things," the mind enters into a deeper stillness. By controlling sensory input, one can attain inner calm and peace. Amma declares, "The thoughts of the mind are like the waves of the ocean. One cannot stop the waves by force. But when the ocean is deep, the waves subside. Similarly, try to concentrate the mind on one thought, instead of trying to stop all thoughts by force. The ocean of the mind will become deeper and it will become quiet. Even if there are small waves on the surface, it will be peaceful." Regular withdrawal of the senses, e.g. through weekly fasting and silence, greatly helps to calm the mind, and one's attachments to the outer world start to diminish. There is a saying in the scriptures that if we cannot control the tongue (speech and food), then it is not possible to control the mind. Fasting and observing silence once a week or every other week is a very useful tool to make the waves of the mind subside.

5

Supplements

Detox Tea

½ tsp. nettles leaf
½ tsp. dandelion root powder
¼ tsp. milk thistle powder
¼ tsp. bhumiamalaki powder
1/8th tsp. punarnava powder
Put the herbs in 2 cups of water and boil down to 1.5 cups.
Turn off heat, cover and let sit for 20 minutes.
Strain the herbs.
Sip warm/hot as a tea 30 minutes before each meal and any time of the day.

Digestive Detox Tea

½ tsp fresh ground cumin seed
½ tsp fresh ground coriander seed
½ tsp fresh ground fennel seed
½ tsp ginger powder or fresh grated ginger root
½ tsp turmeric powder or fresh grated turmeric root
Put the herbs in 1½ cups of water and boil down to 1 cup.
Turn off heat, cover and let sit for 20 minutes.
Strain the herbs.
Sip warm/hot as a tea 30 minutes after each meal and any time of the day if you experience digestive discomfort.

Triphala

Take 3 g *triphala* powder (approximately 1 tsp) 1-2 hours after dinner with a teaspoon of ghee or honey or a cup of hot water or digestive detox tea. If the taste of the powder is too intense, you can use capsules. They usually come in 500 mg capsules, so you would take six.

Triphala means "three fruits," with *tri* meaning "three" and *phala* meaning "fruit." The three fruits contained in triphala are *haritaki, amalaki,* and *bibhitaki.* There is a saying in India that if a *Vaidya* (Ayurvedic practitioner) knows how to skillfully use triphala, he can heal any disease. It is highly revered throughout the history of Ayurveda. When these three fruits are dried and combined as triphala, they form a very powerful *rasayana.* A rasayana is the most highly refined and powerful herbal combination in Ayurveda, and is known to promote long life and rejuvenation. A rasayana promotes *ojas*, the material equivalent of physical immunity and emotional contentment or bliss. On the purely physical level, ojas is also defined as the finest product of digestion, which prevents disease, creates luster in the skin, and rejuvenates the whole body.

Triphala gently cleans toxins out of the digestive track. Triphala is most commonly known for its use as a laxative and can be used to stimulate bowel movements. It cleanses the stomach and ensures clearer bowel movements. Other uses include the relief of flatulence and digestive cramping. It also provides nutrition in the form of nutrients and vitamins to the entire digestive tract, starting from the esophagus to the anus, and it improves and strengthens the rectal muscles. Triphala bolsters many other systems as well. In addition to the GI tract, Ayurveda uses triphala to support healthy respiratory, cardiovascular, urinary, reproductive, and nervous systems. It as well increases liver functions and metabolic support as cleaning the skin Triphala has also been shown to be a powerful antioxidant, protecting cells from the damaging effects of free radicals.

Turmeric

Take 1-2 g of turmeric powder thirty to sixty minutes after each meal. This is best taken with a cup of hot water.

Turmeric is the most researched herb in the world. There are entire books written on turmeric alone. Here are a few of the main health properties of this magical plant: Turmeric, and especially its most active compound curcumin, has the potential to prevent heart disease, Alzheimer's, and cancer. It's a potent anti-inflammatory and antioxidant and may also help improve symptoms of depression and arthritis.

While Ayurveda encourages the use of whole plants over extracts whenever possible, the research on curcumin is indisputable. Ayurveda recommends using turmeric with a small amount of black pepper to activate many of its healing components.

Turmeric also acts as an antioxidant to counter damaging compounds called free radicals and fight oxidative stress. In a nutshell, oxidative stress is stress that occurs when there is an imbalance between the production of cell-damaging free radicals and the body's ability to counter their harmful effects.

Because of turmeric's potent anti-inflammatory and antioxidant benefits, it has health benefits for the skin, preventing or helping to repair visible signs of aging. Turmeric has also been shown to increase levels of neurotrophic factor (BDNF) in the brain, which is crucial, because BDNF acts as a growth hormone that protects the brain from age-related decline or damage. Low BDNF levels are tied to depression and Alzheimer's. Turmeric also has profound blood sugar balancing effects, making it a potent healing agent for those with type-1 or type-2 diabetes. It helps to lower blood-sugar levels and fight insulin resistance.

Turmeric is an amazing support for our organs' natural detoxification systems. It supports the thinning of bile, allowing it to flow more freely through the intestines to eliminate it from the body.

Activated Charcoal

Take 1 g in the evening 2-3 hours after dinner. It is ideal to use activated charcoal sourced from coconut. This is available in powder or capsule form.

Activated charcoal is a natural way to detox and slow down the aging process, as it assists in the removal of deep-seated toxins. Activated charcoal is known for its ability to bind to certain poisons, heavy metals, and other toxins, and flush them from your body, making it an incredible substance for acute and general detoxification. It also carries a host of anti-aging and cardiovascular benefits.

Activated charcoal is the by-product of burning a carbon source like wood or (better yet) coconut shells. The substance is "activated" by high temperatures, removing all the oxygen and changing its chemical structure to create much smaller particles with more surface area. The result is ultra-fine charcoal with millions of tiny pores that capture, bind, and remove poisons, heavy metals, chemicals, and intestinal gases.

Allopathic medicine primarily uses activated charcoal to soak up poisons or other toxins in a hospital or clinical setting. It works through a process called *adsorption* (as opposed to *absorption*), which means "to bind to" rather than "to absorb." Activated charcoal is much more than an antidote for drugs and poisons. It's a universal remedy for general detoxification, digestive health, gas, bloating, and heart health.

Activated charcoal has extremely powerful anti-aging properties. Recent studies show it prevents numerous cellular and mitochondrial changes associated with aging. Activated charcoal slows the rate at which the brain and body becomes sensitive to toxins as we chronologically age. It helps to build better immune defenses by improving the adaptive functioning of essential organs like the liver, kidneys, and adrenals.

Activated charcoal isn't just for use during a detoxification program, it can be consumed on a daily basis. This is an excellent way to help the body in its daily activities in overly toxic modern environments. It prevents the absorption of toxins. It's best to take on an empty stomach and a few hours after a meal or consumption of any vitamin or mineral supplements, as it may interfere with their absorption. Evening time is the best.

Digestive Enzymes

Use a comprehensive digestive enzyme before each meal. There are many high quality herbal based enzymes available on the global market. This will support the digestive process of breaking down food nutrients completely while the body cleanses itself.

Why do we need a digestive enzyme? Digestion is an extremely complex process that begins when we chew food, which releases enzymes in our saliva. Most of the digestion process happens thanks to gastrointestinal fluids that contain digestive enzymes, which are supposed to break down food nutrients (fats, carbs, or proteins). We make specific digestive enzymes to help with absorption of different types of foods we eat. The body makes nutrient specific enzymes such as carbohydrate-specific, protein-specific, and fat-specific enzymes.

Digestive enzymes are essential. They turn complex foods into smaller compounds, including amino acids, fatty acids, cholesterol, simple sugars, and nucleic acids (which make DNA). Enzymes are synthesized and secreted in different parts of the digestive tract, including your mouth, stomach, and pancreas. A large number of people are not able to produce enough enzymes to digest food properly. This undigested food turns into *ama* (metabolic waste) and is the one of the primary causes of disease. Enzyme deficiencies may result from a combination of age, diet, and lifestyle. These deficiencies can lead to a variety of digestive discomforts, including occasional gas, bloating, indigestion, constipation, and irregularity.

It is not recommended to take digestive enzymes indefinitely. They are for re-establishing the digestive process. The body needs to re-learn how to create its own *agni* (digestive fire). The enzymes are beneficial during detoxification programs as the body needs extra support at this time.

Candida

If you suspect or know you have an overgrowth of *Candida albicans*, take an anti-candida formula. Take 2 caps 1 hour before each meal. If you choose to skip dinner, there is no need to take it.

Candida albicans is part of our natural microflora, the microorganisms that commonly live in or on our bodies. It can be found in the GI tract, the mouth, and the vagina. Most of the time it causes no issues, but it's possible for overgrowths and infections to happen. Candida albicans is an opportunistic pathogenic yeast that is a common member of the human gut flora. When gut health is not at optimum conditions, this bacterial yeast overgrows and creates a variety of symptoms and illness. Common symptoms include chronic fatigue syndrome, lethargy, fatigue, mood disorders, brain fog, lack of motivation, most digestive imbalances, thrush, muscle and joint pain, skin and nail fungus or infections, vaginal and urinary tract infections.

Probiotics

A full spectrum probiotic should be taken for 10-21 days after the cleanse to completely recolonize the gut with friendly flora. It is best to use a high quality broad-spectrum probiotic. Usually the ones found in the refrigerator at your local health food store are the best. Most health food stores carry a few really high quality ones. Do some research and take the best available.

6

Ahara (Meal Planning/ Food Therapy)

Eat two to three meals per day at the same time each day. During the cleansing process, the goal is to remind the body how to enter into and maintain a metabolic state. One of the best ways to initiate this process is to eat two to three meals a day, at the same time, without snacking in between. This gives the body a chance to switch to a calm, stable, detoxifying fuel, the body's own fat. The key to success with this is to make lunch your main and largest meal of the day. That doesn't mean overeat. The stomach should never be full. If the stomach is full there is no room for the *agni* (digestive enzymes/ fire) and *prana* (vital air) to break down the food.

During each meal, take time to sit down, relax, and enjoy it, with no newspapers, books, or electronic devices. If possible eat in silence and pay close attention to chewing. It is also good to eat with kind, loving, and good company and calm uplifting conversation. For optimum cleansing results, eat breakfast around 9 a.m., lunch between 12-2 p.m., and dinner (if any) at 5 p.m. This will give your body maximum digestion and cleansing. There are essentially two different meal plans, both involving *kichari*. Kichari is a combination of mung beans and basmati rice cooked together into a porridge-like substance, which forms a complete protein.

Organic Food

Treat the earth well. It was not given to you by your parents, it was loaned to you by your children. We do not inherit the Earth from our Ancestors, we borrow it from our children.

~ Native American Proverb

Many years ago, traditional agriculture used methods that respected nature's rhythms and utilized only substances that nature provided. The widespread use of chemical fertilizers, pesticides, and herbicides in farming has upset nature's balance, threatening the wellbeing of not only our external environment but also the internal environment of our bodies.

Many farmers, having noticed these detrimental effects, have returned to using systems of organic agriculture that increase soil fertility and restore harmony in nature. These systems include the addition of natural inputs such as compost, animal manures, and biodynamic preparations, as well as appropriate crop rotations. Plants grown in well balanced, fertile soils are strong and healthy. They resist disease and pests in the same way that healthy and happy humans resist disease.

Pesticides and chemical fertilizers are not necessary for farming. They are highly destructive to soil life and the health of plants. Residues of toxic pesticides and herbicides, when consumed through our food, accumulate in human body tissue. They also end up in waterways where their impact spreads widely throughout nature. Globally, more than five billion pounds of pesticides are used every year.

Organic food is completely free from all chemicals, and is never irradiated after harvest. To become certified organic, produce must be grown in soil that tests free from heavy metal contamination. There is scientific evidence showing that the accumulation of the aforementioned toxic substances in our bodies can lead to a wide variety of health problems, including impaired immune function, cancer, allergies, autoimmune diseases, impaired fertility, and birth defects. Annually, close to five million people worldwide suffer from symptoms of pesticide poisoning, while ten thousand people actually die each year from these poisons. Studies have shown that the lifespan of conventional commercial farmers is significantly shorter than that of organic farmers.

Currently many non-organic, commercial foods are genetically modified. Genetically modified organisms (GMOs) present a potential danger to humans as well as to the ecosystem. Many species of animals, such as the monarch butterfly, are becoming extinct due to GMOs. For vegetarians, GMOs pose another problem, as they are frequently spliced from animal DNA. It is hypothesized by many experts that GMO food will eventually even alter human DNA. As GMOs are a recent creation, their long-term effects are unknown.

In India and other developing nations, western-based GMO and pesticide companies are aggressively promoting extremely heavy use of chemicals for farming. This is leading to serious soil depletion and water contamination. Many insects are developing stronger resistance to pesticides, and sometimes even huge amounts of chemicals are ineffective. For this reason, many farmers have little or no yield, year after year. Having gone deeply in debt to these chemical companies, the farmers begin to feel hopeless. Tragically, large numbers of Indian farmers are committing suicide by drinking their pesticides. Entire families die on a daily basis. When we choose organic, non-GMO foods, we are doing our part to try to end this horrific situation.

Certified organic food has much higher nutritional content than non-organic food, so the consumer gets more for their money. Many people also find that organic food tastes better. Organic food has higher life force (prana) than commercial food too. Thus, it is clear that eating organic food is a primary step towards personal and global health.

"Nature gives all of Her wealth to human beings. Just as Nature is dedicated to helping us, we too should be dedicated to helping Nature. Only then can the harmony between Nature and humanity be preserved."

~ Amma

Food as Prayer

"Not a grain of the food we eat is made purely by our own effort. What comes to us in the form of food is the toil of our sisters and brothers, and the bounty of Nature and God's compassion. Even if we have a million dollars, we still need food to satisfy our hunger. After all, we cannot eat dollars. So we should never eat anything without first praying with a feeling of humility and gratitude. Consider your food to be the Goddess Lakshmi (the Goddess of Prosperity), and receive it with devotion and reverence. Food is Brahman (the Supreme Being). Eat the food as God's prasad (blessed gift)."

~ Amma

Amma constantly reminds us that we are not the body; we are the *Atman* (the Supreme Self). So why bother to eat healthfully? These bodies are vehicles for transporting the soul. Just as we would not put gasoline mixed with dirt into our cars, we should consider what type of fuel we put into our soul's vehicle. At the same time, we should be careful not to take our diets so seriously that we lose a sense of gratitude for whatever food we receive. Our thoughts and attitude during meals affect our digestion and assimilation as much as the food itself. We are blessed if we have enough food to provide energy and nutrition. Millions of people do not have this. We have profound potential to heal ourselves and Mother Earth by making some simple changes to our dietary habits. Amma again and again reflects to us that Mother Nature is greatly out of balance. She constantly encourages us to help restore that balance. By Her Grace, may we each find that balance internally and externally.

Foods to Avoid

To gain the most benefits from the cleansing process, avoid these foods:

- Genetically engineered/modified foods (GMOs)
- Gluten: wheat, oats, rye, barley
- Dairy, except for ghee made from organic grass-fed butter
- All processed and artificial foods
- White and artificial sugars
- Bread and any type of flour including pastas, muffins, cookies, etc.
- Heavy foods (yogurt, nuts, oils, cheese, pizza)
- Curd, pickles, vinegar
- Soy products (including tofu, tempeh, miso, edamame)
- Raw and uncooked vegetables
- Cold drinks, cold foods, ice
- Alcohol, caffeine, and recreational drugs

Meal Plan One: Kichari Only

Eating only kichari maximizes your body's ability to detoxify and receive the most benefits from the cleanse. This is incredibly healing to the digestive tract and extremely detoxifying. When we eat a mono diet, the body can refocus the energy that normally goes towards digestion to cleansing and healing. This meal plan is a truly transformative option for both the body's detox process and one's psychological relationship to food. Always eat your largest meal midday, when the agni is the strongest. As far as dinner is concerned, eat early and small. The stomach's capacity for food is three cups by volume. That is actually a lot of food. We should really never feel totally full. If we feel full, we have probably overeaten and this leads to sluggish metabolism and toxic build up. Breakfast should be 1-1½ cups of food. Lunch can be 2-2½ cups of food. Dinner should be 0-1 cup of food. If we drink enough warm water during the day this will be plenty of food.

Also take 1 tbsp of extra virgin cold-pressed coconut oil two times a day between the meals. This will further support your body's ability to burn toxins and give you a little more energy.

Meal Plan Two: Kichari with Vegetables

This is basically the same as Meal Plan One, but with cooked vegetables. The vegetables can be steamed or cooked right into the kichari at the end. This plan gives a little more variety and some nutrients that the body doesn't get eating kichari alone. It is not quite as cleansing as eating only kichari but is still incredibly beneficial. Like in the kichari only plan, take 1 tbsp extra virgin cold-pressed coconut oil two times a day between meals.

Quantities
Breakfast: ½-1 cup kichari + ½ cup vegetables
Lunch: 1-1½ cups kichari + ½-1 cup vegetables
Dinner: ½ cup kichari + ½ cup vegetables

Ghee (Clarified Butter)
In Ayurveda, ghee is highly regarded as being one of the most *sattvic* foods. It is beneficial for all three *doshas*, and is the healthiest of all oils. It can be used in any recipe and in place of any oil.

To make ghee, melt one pound of organic grass-fed unsalted butter in a saucepan on medium heat. The better the quality of butter, the better the ghee will be. As the butter melts, it will begin to boil, and white froth will float to the top while sediments settle to the bottom. Do not stir the butter. Ensure that the butter boils evenly by maintaining a consistent temperature. Allow the butter to boil until the bubbling noise becomes quiet, the sediment at the bottom of the pan starts to turn a golden brown (check the color of the sediment by slowly tilting the pot), and the liquid under the froth begins to turn an amber color. This usually takes about 18-20 minutes. Let the cooked ghee cool for 15-20 minutes, then line a fine mesh strainer with cheesecloth and strain the ghee into a sterilized glass jar. Discard the sediment. The ghee will harden when cooled. It is not necessary to refrigerate. If ghee is good quality, it should keep for over a year. Be careful not to get water in the container when using the ghee, or the ghee may spoil.

Tridosha Kichari Recipe

Serves 2

Ingredients

2 tbsp grass-fed ghee (use coconut oil if you are vegan)

½ cup mung dal

½ cup white basmati rice

2 tsp cumin seeds

2 tsp fennel seeds

¼ tsp coriander seeds

5 tbsp freshly grated ginger

1 tsp turmeric powder

⅛ tsp fine black pepper

2-3 pinches hing (asafoetida)

1 heaping tsp Himalaya salt

1 whole onion chopped

1-3 garlic cloves chopped

½ cup cilantro (coriander leaf), chopped

5-6 cups water

Note: You can adjust the quantities and types of spices according to taste, bodily constitution, and season.

Instructions

Wash mung beans and soak in water overnight (6-12 hours).

Wash basmati rice and soak for two hours.

Thoroughly rinse mung beans and basmati rice.

Add 5-6 cups of water in a stainless steel pot. Bring to a boil and add the beans and rice. You may need to add more water as you go.

In a separate heavy-bottomed pan, add ghee on medium heat. This can be done when the mung beans and basmati rice are nearly finished cooking.

Sauté the cumin, fennel, coriander, fresh ginger, and any other herbs (not powdered) in ghee until the seeds start to pop.

Add onions and garlic and cook until slightly golden.

Add the dry spices (turmeric, black pepper, Himalaya salt, and hing) to the pan and sauté for about thirty seconds, not more.

Add all the ghee and herbs to kichari and mix well, infusing the spices into the kichari.

Cook and continue to stir for a few minutes until it is a creamy porridge-like texture. You may need to add more water to get the desired texture.

When the kichari is finished cooking, turn off the heat and add the fresh cilantro. Cover and let sit for 5-10 minutes before serving. You may add Himalaya salt to taste if you like.

Note: If you are following Meal Plan Two and want to mix the vegetables into the kichari, do this when there are five minutes left to cook. If you don't want the vegetables mixed into the kichari, simply steam the veggies. They can be garnished with fresh herbs and ghee or coconut oil.

Vegetables

Make sure that all vegetables are organic. Remember, you are cleansing and detoxing. Non-organic veggies add toxins. The majority of the vegetables should be green, like kale, collards, chard, Swiss chard, mustard greens, arugula, beet leaves, dandelion greens, spinach, watercress, fennel, broccoli, green peas, green beans, celery, asparagus, Brussels sprouts, endives, bok choy, turnip greens, and microgreens like sunflower sprouts and pea sprouts.

The other vegetables can be a variety of colors. The healthiest choices are burdock root, beet root, carrots, red cabbage, sweet potato, yams, seaweeds, cooked onions, zucchini, and cauliflower.

Basic steamed vegetables are enough. If you like you can add ghee or olive oil to them once they are served. You can also use fresh or dried herbs like rosemary, thyme, oregano, dill, basil, tarragon, sage, etc. You may also eat vegetable dishes from the recipe section at the end of this book.

7

Shodhana (Purification)

To eat when you are sick is to feed your sickness.

~ Hippocrates

Instead of using medicine, rather it is better to fast for a day.

~ Plutarch

Hydration

Hot Water – Sipping warm/hot water throughout the day allows the body to stoke the metabolic fire and burn up deep-seated toxins.

Drinking hot water goes far beyond any detoxification program. Daily consumption of hot water is a key to good health and longevity. Drinking hot water replenishes your body's fluids. It can also improve digestion, relieve congestion, and even make you feel more calm, relaxed, and satiated. Most people drink hot water as a health remedy first thing in the morning and again before bed for optimal health benefit. Many add lemon juice, ginger, and/or raw honey to their first glass of the day to enkindle the digestive fire and support peristalsis. Warm water is at least 120°F (48.8°C) and hot water is 140°F (60°C).

Additional Benefits of Drinking Hot Water

Drinking hot water both soothes and activates your digestive tract. Water is the substance that keeps your digestion going. As water moves through the stomach and intestines, digestive organs are properly hydrated and able to eliminate waste. Hot water can also dissolve and dissipate foods that the body might have trouble digesting. Drinking hot water aids in weight loss and alleviates constipation. It also improves circulation and helps to reduce inflammatory stress hormones.

Swedhana (Sweating)

Sweating is an excellent way to easily and quickly rid the body of toxins. It is scientifically proven that sweating is the second most effective method of removing toxins from the body. The first is drinking warm/hot water. Go to a steam sauna or far infrared sauna every third or fourth day. Sweating for 45-60 minutes is ideal. If you are doing a steam sauna, the best way to sweat is in 15 minute increments. After each sweat session, rinse in cold water and rehydrate. Take a 15-20 minute break between each round of sweating. If you are in a far infrared sauna, you can sweat for 30 minutes and do the same process: cold rinse, rehydrate, break, and sweat again. It is a good idea to keep your feet warm. During the resting times it is very beneficial to keep feet in a warm foot bath. Salt and essential oil may ne added to this if you like.

There are countless health benefits associated with regular sweating via steam bath. Regular steam baths improve circulation by dilating the small blood vessels, or capillaries. Blood can then flow more easily and transport oxygen around the body. Steaming has been shown to reduce blood pressure and keep the heart healthy. Steam baths help the body to sweat and remove toxins via the skin. Steam baths and far infrared saunas increase metabolic rate and help to burn white or yellow fat (the unhealthy kind). Steam baths also soothe the nerve endings and relax the muscles. A less well-known benefit of saunas and steam baths is that they can ease joint and headache pain. Regular use of a steam room or sauna can greatly aid in weight loss as it rids the body of water weight. Other benefits are quick muscle recovery after workouts, increased flexibility, heightened sense of well-being, and better-looking skin.

If it isn't possible to sweat via steam sauna or far infrared sauna there is another way: taking a hot herbal bath. Fill the bath with hot water, making sure it is not so hot that you experience dizziness. Add one cup each of dry ginger powder and yellow mustard powder. Before the bath, make 16-32 oz of strong ginger tea with fresh or dry ginger. Drink half before you enter the bath and the other half while in the bath. This should create a nice sweat. Stop if you get dizzy or feel faint.

Ayurveda has used sweating as a primary way of detoxing for thousands of years. This traditionally was done in a sweat box with herbalized steam. Most indigenous traditions around the world used some form of a sweat lodge. The Native American traditions used sweat lodges called *Inipi*. Inipi means "to live again." The sweat lodge is a traditional Native American place of prayer and connecting to Great Spirit (God), our Highest Self. It is used to purify the body and mind and uplift consciousness. It is considered an ancient medicine temple to honor the five elements: Space, Air, Fire, Water, and Earth.

> *When you come out of a purification lodge, you don't feel the same as when you come out of a sauna. The ceremony is a rebirthing process. There's something that happens in a spiritual sense that is powerful and uplifting.*
>
> ~ *William J. Walk Sacred, Cree medicine man*

The Cree word for the purification ceremony is Oenikika, which means the breath of life. It is a process of renewal through the integration of the physical and spiritual.

William Walk Sacred explains, "Just think of this as a marriage ceremony that takes place within yourself. The ceremonial leader is the medicine man. He is a representative of the spirits, who works within the invisible realm, in order for you to become aware of the healing process within yourself."

Detox Bath

2 cups Epsom salt (magnesium sulphate)
1 cup Himalaya or sea salt
2 cups baking soda (sodium bicarbonate)
½-1 cup ground ginger
½-1 cup yellow mustard powder
5 drops lavender essential oil

Make a hot bath, add ingredients, and circulate until fully dissolved. Bathe as warm as possible, and soak for 45 minutes, adding more hot water if the bath cools. You will notice your skin turning red and you will sweat. This is part of the detox. The more ginger you use, the more heat you will experience. Turn the lights out or use a Himalaya salt lamp or a rose quartz or quartz crystal lamp. Listen to soothing and calming music while soaking. After 45 minutes, exit the bath and pat your skin dry with an organic cotton towel.

Virechan (Intestinal Purgation)
Day 5 Intestinal Purgation

It is important to flush out the impurities that have collected in the intestines throughout the cleanse. After purgation, rest for a day. There is no need to exercise on this day other than a gentle walk.

Castor Oil Flush

Ingredients
1-2 oz (30-60 ml) cold-pressed castor oil
3 g triphala (1 tsp of triphala powder or six 500 mg capsules)
Vata types may want to add 4oz. of aloe vera juice as well.
Pitta can take a glass of hot milk with 1-2 tsp. ghee. If you are vegan, or even if you are not, you can also use a tablespoon of Ghandharva Haritaki.

Instructions

The night before the final flush you should have no dinner or a very light dinner. Take the triphala with 16 oz (480 ml) of hot water and go to bed early, before 9 p.m.

Wake up around 4 or 5 a.m. and drink the castor oil along with 16 oz (480 ml) hot water. After taking the castor oil, rest without going back to sleep. This morning, do not apply nasya oil. You can do abhyanga and meditate. You should drink another 16 oz (480 ml) of hot water within the next hour. Wait until the first bowel movement comes. Then continually sip hot water to promote more motions. After each bowel movement, drink another 8-16 oz (240-480 ml) of hot water. Keep drinking hot water and having bowel movements until what you are passing is solely liquid. This may continue until lunch time or early afternoon.

Skip breakfast today and don't eat anything until the laxative effect has worn off.

Lunch should be a very soupy kichari or blended vegetable soup if you have been eating vegetables.

In the evening take a warm (not hot) bath and go to bed early. If you are only doing a 5-day cleanse, on day 6 begin the rejuvenation/reintegration process. If you are doing a longer cleanse, start over as if it were day 1. You would again do this flush on days 10, 15, 20, 25, 30, and 35 depending on the length of your program.

Basti (Enemas) – Caring for Your Colon

It is good for a seeker to purge the stomach at least twice a month. The accumulated feces in the intestines create agitation and negativity in the mind. By purging, we clear not only the body but the mind as well.

~ Amma

Basti (enema) have been used for centuries to relieve constipation and improve general health and well-being, appearing in medical writings as far back as ancient Egypt. Ayurveda and naturopathy acknowledge that health begins with the colon. Illness and disease start with toxins in the colon and spread from there. In addition to fasting, one of the best things we can do to assure good health and a long life is to clean the colon. Please note that during any type of fasting or detoxification, colon cleansing is necessary if there are toxins built up in the colon.

Basti is a mild but deeply therapeutic enema. Basti consists of introducing medicated oils or liquids into the colon to be retained and then released. The primary goal of basti is the purification and rejuvenation of the colon, as the colon is connected to all of the other organs and tissues of the body. There are two main types of basti: cleansing and nutritive. The colon is essential for the absorption of nutrients, and it is also the primary receptacle for waste elimination. It is the seat of vata dosha, which moves the other doshas and all physiological activity. As it balances and nurtures vata, basti has a wide-ranging influence in the body and affects all parts and function of the human body.

Vata's predominant site is the colon. Basti is the most effective treatment of vata disorders, although many enemas over a prescribed period of time are sometimes required. Basti relieves constipation, distention, chronic fever, cold, sexual disorders, kidney stones, heart pain, backache, sciatica, and other pains in the joints. Numerous other vata disorders such as arthritis, rheumatism, gout, muscle spasms, and headaches may also be treated with basti.

Vata is a significant factor in disease pathogenesis. If vata is controlled through the use of basti, the root cause of most diseases can be eliminated. Vata is the primary force behind the elimination and retention of feces, urine, bile, and other excreta.

There are several excellent ways to clean the colon. There are many laxative herbal teas that can be taken in the evening before bed, traditional saltwater flushes, colonics, and enemas. There are colon hydrotherapists available in most cities that can provide 'high colonics,' a machine-administered enema that injects large amounts of fluid high into the colon for cleansing purposes. However, this should only be done during cleansing times and not on any regular schedule. Colonics can actually weaken the musculature and strength of the colon if used on an ongoing basis.

A gentle enema can easily be administered by oneself or with the assistance of a family member or close friend. Ayurveda traditionally uses some form of medicated oil or other substance based on one's unique bodily constitution. While traditional naturopathy also uses oil, it relies heavily on other liquids substances too, such as coffee, baking soda, herbal teas, wheatgrass juice, Epsom salt, Himalaya salt, and sea salt. Fasting in general promotes healthy bowel movements, and other means of colon cleansing should only be administered if the bowels are sluggish or overloaded with excess toxins.

Indications for Basti

Constipation, low-back pain, gout, rheumatism, sciatica, arthritis, auto-intoxication, nervous disorders, vata headache, emaciation, and muscular atrophy

Contraindications for Basti

Diarrhea, rectal bleeding, chronic indigestion, breathlessness, diabetes, fever, emaciation, severe anemia, pulmonary tuberculosis, old age, or children below the age of seven.

Oil enemas should be avoided by people with the following conditions: diabetes, obesity, indigestion, low agni, enlarged liver or spleen, unconsciousness, tuberculosis, and cough.

Decoction enemas should be avoided by people with the following conditions: debility, hiccup, hemorrhoids, inflammation of anus, piles, diarrhea, pregnancy, ascites, diabetes, and some conditions involving painful or difficult breathing.

Nutritional enemas should be avoided by people with the following conditions: diabetes, obesity, lymphatic obstruction, and ascites.

Basti Types

In classical Ayurveda, the types of basti are numerous. They can even be created for specific diseases in specific seasons, which is beyond the scope of this book. Here we review a few types that are usually safe for all.

Oil Basti

A general basti can be made with 1-2 cups (240-500 ml) of plain or medicated oil. Single oils such as ghee and sesame oil can be used safely by anyone. A classic Ayurveda herbal oil formula like Dashamoola thailam or Ashwagandha thailam can be used safely as well. For a deeper cleanse, add 10-30 g of triphala powder to any of the oils.

Liquid Basti

A liquid enema can be performed by administering 16-32 oz (500-1000 ml) of the chosen substance. Many people choose to do a simple water enema. While this is ok, it is more beneficial to add some kind of herbal or plant substance to the enema, the most common being coffee.

Triphala Tea Basti: This can be made with a simple triphala tea. Mix 1ℓ of water and 4 tbsp of triphala powder and bring them to a boil. Remove from heat and cover with a lid and two cotton towels. Let this sit overnight. In the morning, strain the triphala through a fine mesh strainer or cheese cloth. It's fine if there is some powder left in the liquid. Heat the triphala tea to 98-100° F (37.7° C), just slightly above body temperature. Then you are ready.

Wheatgrass Basti: This is a common practice in naturopathy. There are two ways of doing this. One is to just take wheatgrass juice powder and water. Use 4 tbsp of powder per 1ℓ of water. The other way is to juice the wheatgrass fresh, using 4-6 oz (120-180 ml) of juice to 750 ml of water.

Herbal Tea Basti: This is done simply by making an herbal tea. Some of the more common enemas are made as a single herb decoction like licorice root, red clover, burdock root, dandelion root, red raspberry leaf, gentian root, chamomile, or even tulasi. Herbal formulas such as Essiac or any combination of herbs can also be decocted for use in an enema.

Dashamoola Tea Basti: Mix 1ℓ of water and 3-4 tbsp of Dashamoola powder and bring them to a boil. Remove from heat and cover with a lid and two cotton towels. Let this sit overnight. In the morning, strain the powder through a fine mesh strainer or cheese cloth. It's fine if there is some powder left in the liquid. Heat the tea to 98-100° F (37.7° C), just slightly above body temperature. Then you are ready.

Coffee Basti

Coffee basti may be too drying for Vata dosha. It is better if those with Vata constitution use a different type of basti.

Administration of various types of enemas, including coffee enemas, were included in medical and nursing textbooks. (McClain, 1950; A General Practitioner, 1934) Coffee enemas were used in the Merck Manual of Diagnosis and Therapy, a compendium of orthodox medical treatment, through the Twelfth Edition, published in 1972.

Coffee enemas work by stimulating the liver and gallbladder to increase the flow of bile, aiding the liver in its detoxification efforts. In a 1929 paper in the Archives of Internal Medicine, investigators at Lenox Hill Hospital in New York reported that rectal installations of several different liquids caused an increase of bile flow from the liver. In a 2014 study, a group of gastroenterologists used coffee enemas as part of the preparation for video capsule endoscopy (swallowing a capsule with a small camera to photograph the insides of the small intestine). They theorized that coffee enemas would stimulate bile flow, exhausting the supply so that bile would not be present in the intestinal tract to blur the images from the camera. They found that patients who had the coffee enema had better quality images than those who did not, suggesting that the enemas had indeed stimulated the release of bile stored in the gallbladder and bile ducts.

While it might seem strange to inject your morning coffee into your colon, coffee enemas are famous for their detoxification effects. The palmitates in coffee (kahweol and cafestol) enhance the action of glutathione S-transferase, a family of enzymes that play an essential role in the body's natural detoxification process. In addition to cleaning the colon, coffee helps to detoxify the liver and gall bladder as well. Coffee enemas do not pass through the digestive system and do not affect the body the same way as drinking coffee does. When coffee is administered rectally, the hepatic portal veins carry the caffeine directly to the liver. Coffee contains caffeine, theobromine and theophylline, substances that dilate the blood vessels and promote bile flow. Bile is the liquid that is the means through which the liver eliminates stored toxins. Bile (including toxic bile) is reabsorbed nine or ten times by the intestinal walls before it is eliminated through the colon. By using coffee enemas, one assists the elimination of toxic bile from the body.

The coffee enema is also one of the most popular enemas due to its promising effects in alternative cancer treatment. Many renowned modern physicians such as Dr. John Beard, Dr. William Donald Kelley, Dr. Max Gerson and Dr. Nicholas Gonzalez used coffee enemas extensively in the treatment of cancer.

Potential health benefits of coffee enemas
- Boosts immunity
- Increases energy
- Stops yeast overgrowth
- May help in treatment of autoimmune diseases
- Assists in removing parasites from the digestive tract
- Assists in removing heavy metals from the body
- Treats depression
- May help in the treatment of cancer

Coffee Enema Recipe

3 tbsp organic, fair-trade coffee
32 oz (1ℓ) pure, filtered water

After preparing the coffee in a coffee pot, press, or by boiling in a stainless steel pot, let the coffee cool to body temperature before administration. If you are making it in a coffee pot, use non-bleached coffee filters!

Retain the enema for 15-20 minutes if possible.

Cautions and Considerations

The best time to do a coffee enema is the morning. To make certain the cleansing is complete, you may want to administer another smaller (½ℓ or 16 oz) enema four to six hours later. This will remove any bile that was released into the small intestine and not eliminated by the first enema.

Use only organically grown coffee because commercial coffee is loaded with chemicals. The coffee enema goes directly to the liver, and so do any chemicals that were used in the cultivation of that coffee. Avoid coffee enemas in the evening because some individuals still experience effects from the caffeine. Those with sensitivity to caffeine should not take a coffee enema.

If you are new to enemas and don't know how to self-administer one there are numerous explicit and detailed videos available online.

8

Completing the Cleanse and Re-Integrating

After cleansing is complete, it is critical to repopulate the gut with friendly bacteria in order to encourage growth of a healthy microbiome. There are several ways to do this. A great way to do this is to use a probiotic for a week or two as well as making a lassi drink a couple of times a day between meals. This is one of the tastiest and most natural ways to re-populate the gut. Continuing with using triphala long-term is also excellent for building a healthy microbiome. In Ayurveda medicine, triphala is not just a cleanser. It is also a potent rasayana (rejuvenator). Likewise, with turmeric, long term use, whether as a supplement or in your food, provides protection against environmental toxins and aging.

Use this cleansing process as a time to create new and lasting good habits. Continue with your daily routine of self-care and love. Diet should be in harmony with one's unique bodily constitution. There is a constitutional test and food chart at the end of this book. Use it to begin to understand your body's individualized needs.

- Lassi – 2x a day between meals. This is the best natural probiotic.
- Triphala – Triphala is a good formula to use even if your bowel/ elimination is balanced. It is tridoshic and supports ongoing health and vitality. It can be taken in powder or capsule form.
- Turmeric – 1 g after each meal.
- Probiotics – To be taken after a cleanse is complete in order to recolonize friendly flora.

- Dinacharya – These practices can and should be practiced your whole life. They protect the body against toxic buildup and pathogenic invaders.
- Diet – Determine your dosha (bodily constitution) and maintain a diet suitable for your own unique needs.

Staying hydrated and avoiding snacks is a key element in keeping metabolic waste out of the body. The first few meals after cleansing is completed should be light and easy to digest. In fact, if you want to continue eating kichari as a staple indefinitely, it is a great way to maintain optimum digestive health.

Simple Lassi Recipes

Plain Lassi

1 cup water (8 oz or 240 ml)
2-3 tbsp yogurt (coconut yogurt or organic grass-fed cow or goat yogurt)
A pinch of Himalaya salt
A pinch of black pepper (fine ground)
Stir or mix and drink!

Spiced Digestive Lassi

1 cup water (8 oz or 240 ml)
2-3 tbsp yogurt (coconut yogurt or organic grass-fed cow or goat yogurt)
⅛ tsp each of cumin, coriander, and ginger powder
A pinch of Himalaya salt
A pinch of black pepper (fine ground)
Stir or mix and drink!

Sweet Lassi

1 cup water (8 oz or 240 ml)
2-3 tbsp yogurt (coconut yogurt or organic grass-fed cow or goat yogurt)
½ tsp cinnamon

⅛ tsp cardamom
A pinch or two of nutmeg (fine ground)
1 tsp raw coconut or cane sugar (jaggery, sucanat, turbinado) or maple syrup
Stir or mix and drink!

9

What is Naturopathy?

Naturopathy, like Ayurveda, is a philosophy that encompasses a holistic view of life, a model for living a balanced, healthy life. The word "naturopathy" is a Latin-Greek term that can be defined as "being close to or benefiting from nature." Traditional naturopathy does not "diagnose" or "treat diseases," but rather recognizes that the majority of imbalances or degenerative health conditions are due to cumulative lifestyle effects, and that the underlying cause of what we call "disease" is simply improper eating, unhealthy habits, and environmental factors. These cause biological imbalances leading to a weakness of the body's natural immunity and subsequent deterioration and collapse in health.

Traditional naturopathy promotes and teaches natural approaches to health such as fasting and detoxification, right diet, herbs, hydrotherapy, aromatherapy, exercise, rest, and sunshine. Naturopathy uses non-invasive treatments and generally avoids drugs and surgery. It focuses on prevention through naturally-occurring substances, minimally invasive methods, and the promotion of natural healing through cellular rejuvenation and strength.

The Origins of Naturopathy
The principles of naturopathy were employed by the Hippocratic School of Medicine around 400 BC. The Greek philosopher Hippocrates believed in viewing the whole person in regards to finding the cause of disease, and using the laws of nature to induce a cure. It was from this original school of thought that naturopathy takes its principles. Hippocrates said, "Health is the expression of a harmonious balance between various components of man's nature, the

environment, and ways of life – nature is the physician of disease." Human beings are part of nature and the universe, and health is achieved by living in accordance with nature's principles. Harmony is attained through proper nutrition, water treatments, rest, sunshine, cleansing, and fasting. Medicine, religion, and science are intimately related, and humans are seen as a whole – physical, mental, emotional, and spiritual beings in Naturopathic philosophy. The same life force that makes up the universe and nature flows through human beings, and it is the disconnection from this source that causes illness. Early Naturopaths realized that if you could restore the life force of the patient, the body would heal itself.

Foundational Principles of Naturopathy

- The healing power of nature – nature has the innate ability to heal
- Identify and treat the cause – there is always an underlying cause, be it physical, emotional, or psychological
- Do no harm – a Naturopath will never use treatments that may create other conditions
- Treat the whole person – when preparing a treatment plan, all aspects of a person's being are taken into consideration
- The Naturopath as a teacher – a Naturopath educates and empowers the patient to take responsibility for his/her own health by teaching self-care
- Prevention is better than cure – a Naturopath may remove toxic substances and situations from a patient's lifestyle to prevent the onset of further disease

Modern Medicine

While modern medicine has numerous positive and beneficial attributes, it does not subscribe to the idea of holism or to the importance of prevention. In the second century BC, the Yellow Emperor, in The Classics of Internal Medicine, said "A doctor who treats a disease after it has happened is a mediocre doctor, a doctor who treats a disease before it happens is a superior doctor."

In ancient times, Ayurvedic and Chinese physicians were paid to keep their patients healthy and were either dismissed or not paid if the patient became ill. This ensured a health system, not an ill health system, as we currently have with allopathy. Unfortunately this understanding has changed to a new paradigm: Wait until something is broken and then attempt to repair it. This is not intelligent medicine. A major part of naturopathy's goal is educating and empowering the patient to take responsibility for his or her own health. This is not always an easy task in a modern world full of toxins and chemicals.

10

Overview of 5-35 Day Naturopathic Home Cleanse

If following an Ayurvedic meal plan doesn't appeal to you and you still have the desire and/or need to do a deep detoxification program, there is a solution. The programs outlined below still involve the Dinacharya (daily regimen) including supplementation as that is a major component in the detoxification process. However, there are numerous way to "eat" that are more varied and Western-centric. This section outlines a few Westernized food programs you can choose from that will give incredible results. For detailed information on supplementation and purification, please refer to the Ayurveda section of the book. Those processes are the same for both Ayurveda and naturopathy detoxification protocols.

Daily Regimen (Dinacharya)

Wake Up – Rise an hour or more before sunrise. This is the best time for meditation and yoga.
Oral Hygiene – Brush teeth, scrape tongue, and perform *gandusha* (oil pulling).
Abhyanga – Perform self-oilation and massage twice a day.
Nasya – Administer medicated nasal drops throughout the day, once in the morning and again early to mid-afternoon.

Meditation – Sit twice a day, first in the morning and again before bed.

Pranayama – Breathe mindfully.

Exercise – Preferably practice Surya Namaskar (Sun Salutation yoga sequence); Chi Kung, Tai Chi, walking, etc. are also good exercise.

Shodhana (Purification) – *Basti* (Enema) and *swedhana* (Sweating) are powerful ways to remove toxins.

Rest – It is essential to keep all work/social responsibilities to an absolute minimum, if any at all. Avoid all strenuous physical activities and keep physical exertion to a minimum.

Pratyahara (Sensory Withdrawal) – Avoid all external stimuli such as screens (computer, cell phone, iPad, etc.), social media, and television.

Before Bed:

Bath – Take a warm (not too hot) bath with 1-2 cups Epsom Salt and 10-20 drops of lavender essential oil.

Abhyanga – Apply oil to the head, hands and feet. Massage each area for 3-5 minutes.

Sleep – Go to bed before 9:00 p.m. and sleep 7-8 hours.

Ahara (Diet Therapy)

Hydration – Drink at least 3ℓ of pure water every day. Start the day with 500-750 ml of warm water.

Diet
* Take 2-3 specialized meals per day or do juicing .
* Eat organic seasonal vegetables.
* Eat a light breakfast, a medium to large lunch, and a light and early dinner.
* Sip hot water every 10-15 minutes throughout the day.
* If possible and suitable for your constitution, skip dinner.
* Don't snack.

Purification Supplements

Digestive Detox Tea: 1 cup in the morning and evening.
Triphala: 3 g 1-2 hours after dinner with a teaspoon of ghee or honey or a cup of warm water or digestive detox tea. Whether using powder or capsule, Organic India or Banyan Botanicals are great companies.
Turmeric: 1-2 g after each meal.
Activated Charcoal: Take 1 g in the evening 1-2 hours after dinner.
Digestive Enzymes: Use a comprehensive Digestive Enzyme before each meal.
Candida: If you suspect or know you have an overgrowth of *Candida albicans*, take an anti-candida formula. Take 2 caps 1 hour before each meal. If you choose to skip dinner, there is no need to take it.
Probiotics: to be taken after cleansing is complete in order to recolonize friendly flora.

Flushing Out the Toxins

Basti (Enemas): Performing a daily enema with Organic Fair Trade Coffee will assist in removing the toxic waste from the liver and colon.
Detox Baths: There are a couple of different detox baths that can be alternated throughout the cleansing or just stick to one.
Caution: Anyone with chronic conditions, such as high blood pressure or heart conditions, should check with their doctor prior to a cleansing hot bath and begin with a short soak in the tub for just 10-15 minutes, slowly easing into a full session.

Detox Bath 1

2 cups Epsom salt (magnesium sulphate)
1 cup Himalaya or sea salt (use less if you have sensitive skin)
2 cups baking soda (sodium bicarbonate)
½–1 cup ground ginger (use less if you have sensitive skin)
5 drops lavender essential oil

Make a hot bath, add ingredients, and circulate until fully dissolved. Bathe as warm as possible, and soak for 45 minutes, adding more hot water if the bath cools. You will notice your skin turning red and you will begin to sweat. This is part of the detox. The more ginger you use, the more heat you will experience. Turn the lights out or use a Himalaya salt lamp or a rose quartz or quartz crystal lamp. Listen to soothing and calming music while soaking. After 45 minutes, pat the skin dry with an organic cotton towel.

Detox Bath 2

2 cups bentonite clay
1 cup Epsom Salt (magnesium sulphate)
1 cup Himalaya or sea salt
½ cup ground ginger
5 drops lavender essential oil
5 drops rosemary essential oil
5 drops lemon essential oil
Follow same instructions as previous Detox Bath.

11

Naturopathic Meal Plans

During the cleansing process, the goal is to teach the body how to enter into and maintain a metabolic state . One of the best ways to initiate this process is to eat two to three meals a day, at the same time, without snacking in between. This gives the body a chance to switch to a calm, stable, detoxifying fuel: the body's own fat. The key to success with this is to make lunch your main and largest meal of the day. That doesn't mean overeat. The stomach should never be full. If the stomach is full there is no room for the agni (digestive enzymes/fire) and prana (vital air) to break down the food.

During each meal, take time to sit down, relax, and enjoy it, with no newspapers, books, or electronic devices. If possible, eat in silence and pay close attention to chewing. It is also good to eat with kind, loving, and good company, and calm uplifting conversation. During this cleanse do your best to eat your meals at the same time each day. For optimum cleansing results, eat breakfast around 9 a.m., lunch between 12-2 p.m., and dinner (if any) at 5 p.m. This will give your body maximum digestion and cleansing. There are essentially two different meal plans, both involving vegetables. There is an additional plan incorporating fruits as well. All meals should include ¼-1 cup of fresh chopped cilantro. This greatly supports the detoxification process.

Each day, between the meals, have one alkalinizing green juice and one celery juice. This will help to keep the body hydrated and energized while supporting the detoxification process.

Celery Juice: best between breakfast and lunch

12-16 oz celery juice
2 oz cilantro juice
1 oz ginger juice

Green Drink: best between lunch and dinner

12-16 oz celery juice, coconut water, water
30 drops ChlorOxygen
2 oz fresh cilantro juice
1 tsp chlorella powder
1 tsp moringa leaf powder
1 oz fresh ginger juice
1 oz fresh turmeric juice
Stevia to taste (optional)

Meal Plan One

Breakfast

Breakfast (8-10 a.m.): 1-2 cups of vegetables
80-100% of these vegetables should be green! The more bitter greens and dark leafy greens the better. The best green veggies to use are arugula, dandelion, mustard greens, beet leaves, endives, kale, collards, chard, rainbow chard, spinach, celery, broccoli, asparagus, green peas, okra, cucumbers, and micro-greens (sunflower sprouts, radish sprouts, alfalfa sprouts, pea sprouts, fenugreek sprouts, clover sprouts, broccoli sprouts, etc.).

Other vegetables that are excellent to use in this cleanse are burdock root, daikon radish, red cabbage, beets, carrots, parsnips, turnips, onions (cooked only), and seaweeds.

Preparation

There are several excellent ways to prepare your veggies to start the day.

Method 1

Steamed. After steaming, add 1-2 tsp of oil (hemp, olive, sesame, or coconut oil). You may add fresh herbs like rosemary, basil, thyme, oregano, dill, tarragon, etc. You can steam the herbs with the vegetables if you like. You may also add Himalaya salt to taste or coconut liquid amino acids.

Method 2

Blended soup – cooked or raw.
Cooked

If you prefer your soup cooked, prepare the raw version but pour it into a stainless steel pot and heat it on the stove. If you are using coconut oil, you can blend the coconut oil in then. If you are using other oils add them after the soup is done heating. If you have blended it properly for 2-3 minutes, you don't need to bring it to boil. Just make it hot.

Raw

If you are *vata dosha*, it is not recommended that you do a raw meal plan without first consulting a qualified health care practitioner. If you are *pitta* or *kapha* constitution, and it is not the middle of a cold winter, it is fine to do raw. Just make sure there is enough oil in the food so you don't dry out internally.

Take a cup of vegetables and a cup of water plus whatever herbs you want to use and blend it for 2-3 minutes. If you want to have a raw soup simply pour it into a cup and eat. It is good to follow the old nutritional saying, "drink your food and chew your drink." That means swish it around in your mouth for a while to activate the salivary glands and start the enzyme production process.

Method 3

Make juice! In a high quality juicer, make 16-20 oz fresh juice. At the end of this section there are juice recipes and juicer and blender recommendations.

Lunch

Lunch (12-2 p.m.): 2-3 cups of food. 60-70% of the veggies should be green. Lunch should be the biggest meal of the day. Essentially eat as much vegetables as you want here. You can also make your lunch any way you like: raw salad, raw blended soup, steamed, boiled/soup, sautéed, baked, roasted, curried or grilled as long as the temperature of the grill doesn't exceed 350°F (176°C).

Dinner

Dinner (5-7 p.m.): 1-1½ cups of food and any color veggies you like. Dinner should be the smallest and lightest meal of the day. You are already eating pretty light but this should be lighter. Soup makes for a super supper! Adding miso to the soup is a great way to finish the day. Don't forget to add at least a teaspoon of oil at the end.

Meal Plan Two

Meal Plan Two is similar to the first meal plan but incorporates fruit. Remember that all meals should include ¼-1 cup of fresh chopped cilantro. And don't forget your juices between meals!

Breakfast

Breakfast (8-10 a.m.): 1-2 cups of vegetables or fruit

For vegetable preparations follow Meal Plan One guidelines. As far as fruits go, the majority should be red, blue, or purple in color—such as berries, cherries, pomegranates, persimmons, or dragon fruit. While red, blue, and purple fruits are the best, the only fruits not to be used are bananas and melons. Fruit can simply be eaten as is, cooked, or made into a salad or smoothie.

Fruit Salad

1-1½ cups of fruit (basically any 2-3 fruits go well together)
1 tsp coconut oil
1-2 tbsp shredded coconut
1 tsp lemon juice

½ cup chopped cilantro
a pinch of cayenne pepper.

My favorite fruit combos are: pomegranate + blueberries; blueberries + mango; mango + banana; papaya + kiwi; blueberries + blackberries + dark cherries; dark cherries + peaches

Coconut Yogurt with Fruit

1 cup of coconut yogurt
1 cup of fruit (wild blueberries, cherries, and/or mango are my favorite with coconut yogurt)
¼-½ cup chopped cilantro

Cooked Fruit: Stewed apples, pears, peaches, cherries, berries, or apricots

1-2 cups of fruit
1-2 tbsp raw coconut sugar or jaggery
1 oz (30 ml) water

Directions

In a stainless steel pot, add all the ingredients. Mash them together and cook on medium heat for 5-7 minutes. Turn the heat off and cover the pot. Let it sit for 10 minutes. Add ½ cup chopped cilantro.

Options

1. ⅛-¼ tsp each: cinnamon, cardamom, clover, ginger, or nutmeg.
2. 2-3 tbsp shredded coconut

Lunch

Follow instructions in Meal Plan One.

Dinner

Dinner is always optional. Only eat if you are actually hungry. Many people find that the juice and green water is very satisfying and don't need to eat dinner.

Follow instructions in Meal Plan One.

Meal Plan Three

Juice!

Meal Plan Three is basically a juice fast/cleanse. This can be anywhere from five days up to five weeks depending on health needs. One day a week, drink water only if possible. The health benefits of drinking water for a day are virtually unparalleled.

All healing protocols from the dinacharya of the Ayurveda section should be followed closely. Don't undertake a long fast/cleanse without consulting your primary care physician. The end of this section contains a wide variety of juice recipes. Follow these or create your own. If you have a centrifugal juicer, make your vegetable juice fresh each time. If you have a masticating juicer you can make all your juice for the day and store it in airtight glass containers in the refrigerator. During the juice cleanse consume the green drink 2 times a day. It can be taken 1-2 hours before breakfast as well as between meals. Drink the juice 3-5 times on a regular schedule.

All juice should include 1-2 oz of cilantro juice and 1 oz ginger juice

16 oz vegetable juice or fruit juice (only drink fruit juice 1-2 times a day)

Example of juice timings: 8 a.m., noon, 4 p.m., 6 p.m.

Green drink (between meals): 10 a.m. and 2 p.m.

Deep DivecDetox

The Deep Dive Detox is for those who have the time and space to really go deep into the cleansing process. This is especially good for those who want to cleanse more than just the physical body. This process allows the space to cleanse unwanted, outdated mental and emotional constructs. It is a process of deep rest and renewal on every level. In addition to cleaning the body, this cleanse asks us to do a deep evaluation of our thought processes and beliefs. The Deep Dive Detox provides a safe construct to release anything not serving our highest Self. This can be done for anywhere from 5 -30 days like the other cleanses.

Deep Dive Detox Overview

• Silence – Silence is a big component of this cleanse. It allows us to be with and examine our thoughts with a deeper clarity. This process allows us to be with Ourself!

• Atma Vicharya (Self-Inquiry) – One of Ayurveda's main tenets is to attain Sat Chid Ananda (Truth – Pure Consciousness – Bliss). This means abiding in the True Self, Pure Awareness. Atma Vicharya allows us to examine the outdated mental patterns that prevent us from being. This Self–inquiry allows us to remove the *Manas Ama* (mental toxins) in a transformative way that is lasting. This is a crucial part of physical, mental, emotional and spiritual transformation and growth.

• Tune in by turning off – Turn off the cell phone, the television, the computer and wifi signal. If you have a "smart" house, turn the applications off. You can go really really deep with this process and even turn off the lights. You can use candles, oil lamps or if needed Himalaya Salt lamps.

• Ahara Rasa – (Diet Therapy) Kichari Only! On this program you will eat only two meals a day.

• Hydration – Drink warm to hot water throughtout the day along with herbal teas.

• Sadhana – Asana, Pranayama, Meditation, Mantra Japa and Atma Vicharya

• Castor Oil Flush – This will be done on the 4th night only, the night before the enema.

• Basti (Enemas): Enema to assist in removing toxins from the g.i. tract. This will be done on day 5. On this day perform an enema as described in the book. You will not take the ghee on this morning. Also it is best to take the day off from the Asana practice. You still

do the other practices after the enema is complete. It is a day of rest and relaxation. It is good to still take an afternoon or evening walk.
• Extended Cleansing: If you are doing a cleanse longer than five days repeat castor oil on night nine and enema on day ten.

Daily Schedule

Morning Routine:

5 - 6 AM – Rise
• Wash face, brush teeth, scrape tongue
• Drink one cup of warm water
• Dry skin brush, take a shower and apply abhayanga oil.

6 - 7 AM
• Ghee – Take 3 TBS of Organic Grass Fed Ghee within one hour of awakening.
• Rest and Digest for 15-30 minutes.
• Atma Vicharya

7 - 10 AM
• Asana – Gentle Surya Namaskar + Savasana (10 minute) 30 - 60 minutes
• Pranayama – Apply nasya oil first, then do Anuloma Viloma (15 - 30 minutes)
• Mantra Japa – 30 - 60 minutes
• Meditation – 30 – 45 minutes

10 - 11:30 AM
Kichari – Prepare the kichari for the day and relax

11:30 - 12 PM
Detox Tea – Drink Detox Tea 30-60 minutes before lunch

12 - 2 PM
• Lunch – Eat 1 ½ - 2 cups of kichari
• After lunch sit for 15 - 20 minutes in gratitude and awareness.
• Breath gently and slowly into the belly.

- Do the dishes and go for a gentle, thirty minute walk.
- Digestive Detox Tea – Drink 30-60 minutes after lunch

2 – 4 PM
- Asana – Gentle Surya Namaskar + Savasana (10 minute) 20 minutes
- Pranayama – Apply nasya oil first, then do Anuloma Viloma (20 minutes)
- Mantra Japa - 20 minutes
- Meditation – 30 minutes

4 – 5 PM
- Read a spiritual book or go for a gentle walk, sit outside if weather permits.

5 – 7 PM
- Detox Tea – Drink Detox Tea 30-60 minutes before diner.

5-6 PM
- Diner – eat 1- 1 ½ cups of kichari
- After diner sit for 15 minutes in gratitude and awareness.
- Breath gently and slowly into the belly.
- Do the dishes and go for a gentle 20-30 minute walk.
- Digestive Detox Tea – Drink 30-60 minutes after diner.

7 - 9 PM
- Triphala
- Abhayanga
- Bath
- Mantra Japa
- Meditation
- Atma Vicharya/Journal

9 PM
- Bed

Atma Vicharya (Self-Inquiry)

The process of Atma Vicharya allows us the space to examine our mental and emotion processes as well as our consciousness. I would recommend writing in a journal as this allows you a much deeper reflection into your Self. It also provides to framework to examine on how much the mind and emotions changes throughout the healing process. Writing makes it tangible and real.

1. Self Awareness:
In your day-to-day life how much of your time is spent in awareness of your true Self? Asking the question, "Who Am I"? What are my ultimate goals in life? What are my deepest prayers and aspirations? Am I actively making self-effort to achieve these goals and aspirations?

2. Sadhana:
How much time do you dedicate to your spiritual practices (yoga, meditation, mantra, selfless service, etc.)?

3. Natural Awareness:
Every day spend some time in nature cultivating awareness. Use the five senses. Listen to the sounds, feel the earth and the plants, observe the colors, inhale deeply.

4. Mental Awareness:
What thoughts distract me the most? Money, Food, Job, Relationships, News, Social Media, World Events? Does focusing on these things help or hinder me from being in the present moment?

5. Create a new plan:
Create a plan to replace the hindrances with something helpful. Decide what your real goals are and make conscious effort to achieve them. Replace the old, outdated thought or pattern with a new positive one.

6. Look within:
How much time do you spend thinking about what other people are doing? Wishing that other people would be different or change?

That situations were different or would change? Do you judge others or situations? What steps can you take to let go of these patterns?

7. Love:

Are you giving the love you wish to receive? Are you "being" the change that you wish to see in the world? If the answer is no, what can you do to be more Loving? How can you more consciously offer your gifts to the world?

8. Gratitude:

Everyday express gratitude. This can be as simple as writing in your journal three things you are grateful for. It can be the same thing every day or something totally new.

9. Action:

Make a plan of action. When you are done with your cleanse how are you going to be in the world? How will you act with more love, more compassion, more understanding and more in alignment with your purpose in Life.

12

Naturopathic Heavy Metal Detox

Daily Routine

It is highly important to create a daily routine of self-nurturing, love and inner stillness. Reducing stress physically, mentally and emotionally is crucial! For more detailed information on the daily routine and how to implement these see the Ayurveda detox section.

Daily Routine and Practice of Self-Care

Abhyanga – Self-massage with warm sesame oil and warm bath with 1-2 cups Epsom salt. Let the oil sit on your body for 20-30 minutes before the bath. Don't wash the oil off with soap. Instead, use a washcloth or natural sponge to wash it off.

Sleep – 6-8 hours is ideal. Try to go to sleep around 9 p.m., at the latest 10 p.m.

Meditation – 20-30 minutes a day.

Pranayama – Anuloma Viloma, Brahmari, and Omkara Japa 20-30 minutes 2-3 times a day. Upon rising and before bed are most important.

Exercise – Yoga, Tai Chi, Chi Kung, dancing, hiking, walking, and swimming.

Daily Detox Bath – This can be done twice a day if you feel strong enough.

Sensory Withdraw – Avoid TV, newspapers, social media, cell phones, computers, and other electronics as much as possible.

Diet

- Eliminate:
- All animal proteins
- Eggs, fish, and dairy (except ghee)
- Tobacco
- Alcohol
- Coffee
- Black tea
- Gluten: wheat, oats, rye, barley
- Corn
- Chickpeas, lima beans, fava beans, navy beans, pinto beans
- Peanuts, cashews, Brazil nuts, hazelnuts, filberts, pine nuts
- Mushrooms
- Nightshades: tomato, potato, bell pepper, eggplant
- Green/white cabbage, Brussels sprouts
- White sugar, artificial sugar, commercial brown sugar, agave syrup, cooked honey
- All forms of refined, processed foods, such as simple sugars, breads, grain pasta, flours
- Refined Oils: canola, palm, sunflower, safflower

What to Eat

Green Drink: 3 times a day: upon rising, between breakfast and lunch and 2-3 hours before bed. This is profoundly cleansing and removes deep-seated environmental toxins including heavy metals, mold, and other carcinogens.

12-16 oz celery juice, coconut water, water

2 oz aloe vera juice

1 oz pomegranate juice concentrate

30 drops ChlorOxygen

2 oz fresh cilantro juice

1 tsp chlorella

1 oz fresh ginger juice

1 oz fresh turmeric juice

Stevia to taste (optional)

Whole Foods

Put fresh green cilantro (coriander leaf) with everything! Every meal! ½-1 cup per meal.

Oils

For cooking: ghee and coconut oil

On food: ghee, coconut, hemp, olive, or sesame oils. UDO's 3-6-9 is a combination of most of the above

Seeds

2-4 tbsp per meal (not with fruit!). Eat whole/raw, sprouted, seed butter, seed cheese, and seed milks (hemp is the best), including hemp tofu! Pumpkin, sunflower, and sesame. Flax and chia are to be sprouted or freshly ground.

Nuts

Almonds (soaked and peeled if eating raw!) Max 10 total in 24 hours Macadamia (5-7 per day)

Grains

Minimal amounts of whole soaked and/or sprouted and cooked only: quinoa, amaranth, sprouted buckwheat, long grain rice (basmati). The best way to take grains is in kichari.

Beans

Soaked a minimum of 12-24 hours. Sprouted is best then very well cooked: mung, adzuki, red and yellow lentils.

Vegetables

80-90% of the veggies should be green and cooked

Arugula, beet greens, chard, kale, collards, broccoli, dandelion, mustard okra, green peas, kohlrabi, spinach, celery, asparagus, zucchini, fennel, green sprouts (fenugreek, broccoli, radish, clover, mung, pumpkin, chia, sunflower, pea, fenugreek, etc.).

10-20% all the other vegetables

Most important are: cooked onions, burdock root, daikon radish, beets, purple cabbage (esp. juiced with celery), and seaweed (not from Japan!).

OK: carrots, parsnips, turnips, rutabaga, sweet potato, yams, squash, and pumpkin.

Fruits

Do not eat fruit with any other type of food! The exceptions are avocado, olives, and coconut, which can go with anything. It is ok to mix fruits with other fruits except melons. They don't even go with other melons! Fruit must be eaten at least 90 minutes before, or two hours after any other type of food.

Best fruits: 80-90% red, blue, or purple: wild blueberries, pomegranates, berries, persimmons, cherries, plums, dragon fruit, red grapes, red apples, etc.

Spices

Turmeric, fresh ginger, cumin, coriander, fennel, rosemary, thyme, oregano, basil, dill, tarragon, sage, black pepper, roasted garlic, and Himalaya salt.

All spices are ok, these are the best!

Caffeine

If you need to you can still have small amounts caffeine in a form that is healthy and supportive. For example:

• Raw Cacao Tea: 1-3 tsp raw cacao powder + 12-16 oz almond, hemp, flax, or coconut milk + ¼ tsp cinnamon + ½ tsp each turmeric and ginger + 1 tsp unrefined organic raw coconut oil – bring to a boil. Steep 10 min. Add stevia

• Other Antioxidant Caffeinated Tea: Matcha and organic green tea

Meal Planning

All meals except fruit are cooked with rosemary, thyme, and oregano. Other spices are beneficial too but these are the most important!
Eat meals at the same time each day. Breakfast 8-10 a.m., Lunch 12-2 p.m., Dinner 5-6:30 p.m. Dinner should be finished before 7 p.m. Don't eat solid food after 7 p.m.!

Breakfast

Breakfast (8-10 a.m.) 1-2 cups of food.

The best breakfast is either a complete protein with vegetables or fruit by itself. If you are doing the protein and vegetable option, the ratio should be about 30% protein and 70% vegetables. This is by volume not calorie count.

Protein

Kichari (mung beans and basmati rice or other grain cooked together), tempeh, adzuki bean tempeh, Hempeh (hemp tempeh) sprouted tofu, hemp tofu, beans, quinoa, seeds, seed cheese, seed butter, seed pate

Vegetables

Steamed, boiled, sautéed, baked, curried, grilled

or

Fruit

Cooked (baked or stewed), as is, salad, smoothie, or with coconut yogurt

Fruit salad (1 cup of fruit, especially pomegranate and wild blueberries with ½-1 cup chopped cilantro, 1 tbsp coconut oil, 1 tsp lemon and a pinch of cayenne). Other fruits such as blackberries, cherries, and persimmons are wonderful in salads as well. This is also delicious with 1 tbsp of shredded coconut!

Coconut yogurt with fruit and cilantro

Smoothie (1-2 cups coconut milk or water + ½-1 cup fruit + 1 tbsp coconut oil + 2 tbsp coconut yogurt + 1 tbsp spirulina + 1 tsp moringa + 1 tsp chlorella + ½ cup cilantro)

or

Coconut yogurt with seeds, cilantro, flax or hemp seed oil, spices (cinnamon, ginger, cardamom, black pepper, turmeric)

Lunch

Lunch should be eaten between 12-2 p.m. and only 2-2½ cups of food. The best lunch is a complete protein with vegetables. The ratio should ideally be around 50% protein and 50% vegetables.

Protein

Kichari (mung beans and basmati rice or other grain cooked together), tempeh, adzuki bean tempeh, Hempeh (hemp tempeh) sprouted tofu, hemp tofu, beans, quinoa, seeds, seed cheese, seed butter, seed paté, chopped nuts, almond feta cheese

Vegetables

Steamed, boiled, sautéed, baked, curried, grilled

Raw salad in the summer is ok with lots of oil, seeds, and nuts! Bitter greens, spring greens, spinach, sprouts with some grated beets, carrots, daikon radish, and purple sauerkraut. Use lots of seeds/seed cheese and/or chopped nuts, plus 1-2 tbsp oil (hemp, flax, evening primrose, borage, olive) and herbs (rosemary, basil, oregano, thyme, etc.).

Dinner

Dinner should be eaten between 5-6:30 p.m. It should be finished by 7 p.m. at the latest. If possible, skip dinner. The best dinner is vegetables only! Vegetables should be in the form of soup or salad, steamed, curried, baked, or sautéed (similar to lunch but without the seeds and nuts). The other option is to drink vegetable juice.

Dinner Juice

12 oz celery juice

2 oz each spinach, chard or beet leaves, kale, arugula, parsley, cilantro

2 oz red cabbage juice

1 oz each ginger and turmeric

Supplementation

Vitamin B12: 5000 mcg daily, 1-2 hours after breakfast.

Vitamin B6: 500 mg, 1-2 hours after breakfast.

Vitamin C: (Acerola or Liposomal) 1000mg. 1-2 hours after breakfast

Vitamin D3 with Vitamin K2: 2000-4000 IU daily, 1-2 hours after breakfast.

Alpha Lipoic Acid: 500-600 mg after meals.

Digestive Enzyme

Candida Formula

Herbs

Ashwagandha: 2 g (4-500 mg capsules or 1 tsp powder) 3x/day, 1 hour after food
Triphala: 1 g 2x/day empty stomach, morning and evening
Turmeric with black pepper: 3000 mg 2x/day, morning and evening
Activated charcoal: Take 1 g in the evening 2-3 hours after dinner. I recommend using activated charcoal sourced from coconut. This is available in powder or capsule form.
Herbal teas: Lion's mane, cordyceps, reishi, tulasi, rhodiola, nettles, red clover, burdock root, and red raspberry leaf.

Purification

Coffee Enema: Every other day for the first four weeks, then every third day for four weeks, then twice a week after that.
Sweat
Far Infrared Sauna: 30-45 minutes daily.
Steam Sauna: 2x/week (not on enema day) – Total sweat time should be about one hour. Sweat for 10-15 minutes, then take a cold shower and rehydrate, rest 5-10 minutes. Repeat 4-6 times.
Always finish with a cold shower.

13

The Recipes

Yo, Juice Me! Juice Shots

These can be taken straight or diluted in water.

1½ oz cilantro, parsley, wheatgrass, or kale with a pinch of cayenne

Energizing Green Water I

12 oz water or coconut water
1 oz each cilantro, parsley, ginger

Energizing Green Water II

16 oz water or coconut water
3 g each chlorella and spirulina
1 tsp raw honey

Energizing Green Water III

14 oz water or coconut water
½ g each chlorella, spirulina, moringa, barley, alfalfa grass
1 tsp raw honey or stevia to taste

Back to Basics

8 oz carrot
6 oz celery
2 oz cilantro
1 oz ginger

Just Good Juice

8 oz celery
4 oz cucumber
2 oz kale

1 oz each ginger and spinach

Crazy for Kale

8 oz celery
4 oz kale
2 oz spinach
1 oz each ginger, cilantro, turmeric

Ya Know You Want It

4 oz each carrot, celery, beet
1 oz each ginger and cilantro

Ya Know You Want Some More

4 oz each carrot and celery
1 oz ginger, turmeric, cilantro
½ g each spirulina, chlorella, moringa

Chill Out!

8 oz celery
4 oz cucumber
1 oz each cilantro and parsley
3-4 mint leaves

Oh Baby!

8 oz apple
4 oz celery
2 oz lemon
1 oz each ginger, cilantro, parsley
pinch of cayenne

A Green Supreme

8 oz celery
1 oz each kale, collards, spinach, chard, cilantro, parsley, ginger

A Green Supreme (Reprise)

5 oz each carrot and celery
2 oz cucumber

1 oz each kale, spinach, chard, cilantro, ginger

Anytime Antioxidant I

9 oz pomegranate
4 oz apple +
2 oz cherry
1 oz each cilantro, parsley, ginger
(optional: a pinch of cayenne)

Anytime Antioxidant II

8 oz apple
1 oz each red grape, cherry, cilantro, parsley, turmeric, ginger
(optional: a pinch of cayenne)

Love Your Liver Juice

8 oz celery
2 oz each carrot, watercress, and arugula or dandelion greens
1 oz each cilantro and parsley
(optional: ½ g each wheatgrass, alfalfa, and barley powders)

Build Your Blood Juice

5 oz each carrot and beet
2 oz red cabbage
1 oz each ginger, cilantro, parsley
½ g each chlorella and spirulina (or 1 g spirulina)
pinch of cayenne

Re-Hydrate Your Cells

8 oz apple
4 oz lemon
2 oz each cilantro and parsley
pinch of cayenne

Shakti's Super Salad Juice

8 oz celery
2 oz each carrot, beet, parsnip

1 oz each cilantro, burdock, ginger

Vit. B – (Big) Up Yourself

6 oz celery
2 oz each burdock root, beet greens, kale
1 oz each ginger and cilantro

Fat/Calorie Burn

6 oz grapefruit
3 oz orange
2 oz each lemon or lime, cilantro, ginger
1 oz parsley
pinch of cayenne
1 tsp raw honey

Saved by the Spinach

4 oz each celery and spinach
2 oz each beet and carrot
1 oz each cilantro and ginger

Blood Cleanse

5 oz red cabbage
4 oz beet
3 oz celery
1 oz each burdock, daikon, cilantro, ginger, turmeric

Sippin' on Shakti

8 oz pineapple
4 oz orange
2 oz each lemon or lime and ginger
1 oz turmeric
a pinch or two of cayenne

Vegetable Dishes

Salads

Edible Enlightenment Veggie Salad
Serves 4-5
Ingredients
½ cup alfalfa sprouts
½ cup clover sprouts
½ cup bean sprouts
½ cup radish sprouts
¼ cup beets, grated
¼ cup carrots, grated
¼ cup tomato, chopped
¼ cup parsnips, grated
¼ cup red cabbage, chopped
¼ cup celery, chopped
¼ cup green onions, chopped
¼ cup green peas
1 inch ginger, grated
¼ cup almonds, chopped or put through a food processor
1 tbsp de-shelled hemp seeds
½–1 tsp sea salt or to taste or 1 tsp Braggs Liquid Amino Acids
½–1 tsp black pepper fresh ground
1½ tbsp nutritional yeast flakes
1 tbsp fresh cilantro, chopped
1 tbsp fresh basil, chopped
1 tsp fresh mint, chopped
1 tbsp fresh dill, chopped
½ tsp fresh tarragon or ¼ tsp dry
2 tbsp fresh squeezed lemon juice
1 tbsp organic extra virgin olive oil
1 tbsp organic apple cider vinegar or red wine vinegar

Instructions

Mix all the ingredients in a large bowl. Stir for several minutes. Cover and let sit for five minutes.

Great Green Goddess Salad

Serves 4-5

Ingredients

1 cup spinach, chopped

½ cup kale, chopped

¼ cup mustard greens, chopped

½ cup green chard, chopped

¼ cup collard greens, chopped

¼ cup bok choy, chopped

¼ cup dandelion greens, chopped

½ cup alfalfa sprouts

¼ cup celery, chopped

¼ cup green onions, chopped

¼ cup green peas

1 tsp pumpkin seeds

1 tsp crushed or chopped almonds

½–1 tsp sea salt or to taste or 1 tsp Braggs Liquid Amino Acids or Coconut Amino Acids

½–1 tsp black pepper fresh ground

1½ tbsp nutritional yeast flakes

1 tbsp fresh cilantro, chopped

1 tbsp fresh basil, chopped

1 tsp fresh mint, chopped

1 tbsp fresh dill, chopped

½ tsp fresh tarragon or ¼ tsp dry

2 tbsp fresh squeezed lemon juice

1 tbsp extra virgin olive oil

1 tbsp organic apple cider vinegar or red wine vinegar

Instructions

Mix all the ingredients in a large bowl. Stir for several minutes. Add a little water if necessary to make slightly wet. Cover and let sit for five minutes.

Seaweed Supreme Salad

Serves 3-4

Ingredients

¼ cup dulse

½ cup agar

¼ cup arame

¼ cup hiziki

½ cup carrots, grated

½ cup beets, grated

½ tsp organic raw sugar (coconut, sucanat, turbinado, rapidura, etc)

½–1 tsp black pepper fresh ground

2 tbsp fresh cilantro, chopped

1 tbsp fresh basil, chopped

1 tsp fresh mint, chopped

1 tsp fresh or dried rosemary

1 tsp fresh dill, chopped

½ tsp fresh tarragon or ¼ tsp dry

2 tsp fresh squeezed lemon juice

2 tsp balsamic vinegar or apple cider vinegar

2 tbsp water

1 tbsp extra virgin olive oil, hemp, or sesame

Instructions:

Wash the seaweed and soak in fresh water for 20 minutes. Rinse the seaweed again. Mix all the ingredients in a large bowl. Stir for several minutes. Cover and let sit for five minutes.

Anytime Arugula Salad

Serves 2-3

Ingredients

2 cups arugula

½ cup sunflower sprouts

½ cup pea sprouts

½ cup broccoli, clover, or radish sprouts

1 tsp fresh or dried rosemary

1 tsp fresh dill, chopped

½ tsp fresh tarragon or ¼ tsp dry

2 tsp fresh squeezed lemon juice

2 tsp balsamic vinegar or apple cider vinegar

2 tbsp water

1 tbsp extra virgin olive oil, hemp, or sesame

Instructions

Mix all the ingredients in a large bowl. Stir for several minutes. Cover and let sit for five minutes.

Seaweed and Sprouted Seed Salad

Serves 3-4

Ingredients

2 cups alaria or wakame

½ cup arame

3 tbsp hemp seeds

2 tbsp sprouted pumpkin seeds

1 tbsp sprouted sunflower seeds

½ tsp organic raw sugar (coconut, sucanat, turbinado, rapidura, etc)

½–1 tsp black pepper fresh ground

2 tbsp fresh cilantro, chopped

1 tbsp fresh basil, chopped

1 tsp fresh mint, chopped

1 tbsp fresh dill, chopped

½ tsp fresh tarragon or ¼ tsp dry

2 tsp fresh squeezed lemon juice

2 tsp balsamic vinegar or apple cider vinegar

2 tbsp water

1 tbsp extra virgin olive oil, hemp, flax, or sesame oil

Instructions

Wash the seaweed and soak in fresh water for 20 minutes. Rinse the seaweed again. Mix all the ingredients in a large bowl. Stir for several minutes. Cover and let sit for five minutes.

Carrot Cucumber Salad

Serves 2-3
Ingredients
2 cups grated carrots
½ cup cucumber, chopped into small pieces
½–1 tsp sea salt or to taste
½–1 tsp black pepper fresh ground
1 tbsp fresh cilantro, chopped
1 tbsp fresh basil, chopped
1 tsp fresh mint, chopped
1 tsp fresh dill, chopped
½ tsp fresh tarragon or ¼ tsp dry
2 tsp fresh squeezed lemon juice
2 tsp balsamic vinegar
1 tsp nutritional flakes
1 tsp de-shelled hemp seeds
2 tbsp water
1 tbsp hemp seed oil or extra virgin olive oil

Instructions

Mix all the ingredients in a large bowl. Stir for several minutes. Cover and let sit for five minutes.

Rainbow Salad

Serves 4-5
Ingredients
1 cup beets, grated
2 cups spinach, chopped
1 cup carrots, grated
10 black olives sliced
4-5 whole artichoke hearts sliced in halves or quarters

3 small bell peppers thinly sliced lengthwise: 1 green, 1 yellow,
3 tbsp sundried tomato, chopped
1 stalk of celery, chopped
½–1 tsp sea salt or to taste
½–1 tsp black pepper fresh ground
¼ tsp cumin powder
1 tsp de-shelled hemp seed
1 tsp pumpkin seed
1 tbsp balsamic vinegar
1 tbsp fresh squeezed lemon juice
1 tsp nutritional yeast flakes
1 tbsp hemp seed oil or extra virgin olive oil

Instructions

Mix all the ingredients in a large bowl. Stir for several minutes.
Cover and let sit for five minutes.

Summertime Sunflower Salad

Serves 3

Ingredients

2 cups fresh sunflower sprouts
½ cup long mung bean sprouts
2 tbsp sunflower seeds
¼ cup grated carrots
¼ cup celery
2 tbsp cilantro, chopped
1 tbsp parsley, chopped
1 tsp dill (fresh or dry)
1 tbsp balsamic, red wine or apple cider vinegar
1 tsp organic cane sugar
1 tsp hemp, olive, or sesame oil (or ⅓ tsp of each)
1 tbsp fresh squeezed lemon juice

Instructions

Mix everything together in a bowl. Cover and let sit for 10 minutes.

Spice is Nice Salad

Serves 3-4

Ingredients

1 large red cabbage, finely chopped

1-12" daikon radish, grated

1 medium carrot, grated

1" fresh grated ginger

2 small or 1 large hot chili pepper, finely chopped

1 tbsp shredded coconut

1 tbsp fresh squeezed lemon

¼ cup fresh cilantro

1 tsp dill (fresh or dry)

1 tbsp balsamic or apple cider vinegar

1 tsp organic cane sugar

¼ tsp cumin

3 tbsp water

1 tbsp hemp, sesame, or olive oil

Instructions

Mix all the ingredients in a large bowl. Stir for several minutes. Add a little water if necessary to make moist. Cover and let sit for five minutes.

Soups

Soup from Heaven

Serves 3-4

Ingredients

1 cup carrots, chopped into small, thin rounds

1 cup asparagus, chopped

1 cup beets, chopped

1 tsp ginger grated

½ tsp sea salt or to taste

¼ tsp black pepper

½ tsp cumin powder
½ tsp coriander powder
¼ tsp cayenne pepper
1 tbsp garlic minced
2 tbsp ghee or coconut oil
1 tsp cilantro, chopped
3 cups water

Instructions

Heat the ghee on medium heat in a pot and sauté the spices and vegetables (except cilantro) for 4-5 minutes. Add water and bring to a boil. Reduce heat to low and simmer covered for about 25 minutes, stirring occasionally, until the vegetables are soft. Remove from heat, mix in the cilantro and cover. Let sit for 10 minutes and serve.

Spinach Cilantro Ginger Soup

Serves 2-3

Ingredients

1 cup spinach, chopped
1 cup cilantro, chopped
4 oz ginger grated
½ tsp cumin seeds
1 tsp turmeric powder
2 tbsp ghee or coconut oil
¼-½ tsp Himalaya salt or to taste
¼ tsp coriander powder
½ tsp black pepper fresh ground
10 oz coconut milk
2 cups water

Instructions

Grate the ginger and mash it into a paste in a bowl. Heat the ghee or coconut oil and sauté cumin seeds and ginger together. Add turmeric, black pepper, salt, and water. When the water boils, add coconut milk and spinach. Bring to a boil and reduce to low heat. Cook for about 3-4 minutes, stirring frequently to prevent boiling over. Remove from heat and add cilantro. Cover and let sit for 10 minutes. Add salt to taste if needed.

Tahini Miso Onion Soup
Serves 6
Ingredients
1 tbsp coconut oil or grass-fed ghee
6 large white or yellow onions, chopped into small pieces
4 large red onions
2 cloves garlic, grated
1 tsp ginger grated
2 tbsp lemon juice
¼ cup (65g) tahini
3 tbsp tamari (wheat free, non-GMO) or 1 tbsp Himalaya salt
¼ cup nutritional yeast flakes
¼ tsp cayenne pepper
1 tsp rosemary
½ tsp black pepper
3½ cups (825 ml) water
3 tbsp white or red miso paste
2 cups spinach
½ cup cilantro, chopped
Instructions
In a large stainless steel pot bring the water to a boil. Turn the heat down to medium. Add all of the ingredients except for cilantro and miso. Cover and let simmer for 15-20 minutes. Remove from heat and add miso and cilantro. Cover and let sit for 10 more minutes. Ready to serve.

Succulent Seaweed Soup
Serves 3-4
Ingredients
¼ cup dulse
½ cup agar
¼ cup arame

¼ cup hiziki
½ cup grated parsnips
½ cup beets, grated
4-5 cups water
1 tsp black pepper fresh ground
2 tbsp fresh cilantro, chopped
1 tbsp fresh basil, chopped
1 tsp cumin powder
1 tsp fresh dill, chopped
½ tsp fresh tarragon or ¼ tsp dry
1 tbsp coconut oil or ghee
¼ tsp Himalaya or sea salt to taste

Instructions

Bring water to a boil. Add seaweed, beets, and parsnips. Cook for 5-7 minutes. Add all other ingredients and cook for a few more minutes. Remove from heat, cover and let sit for 5 minutes.

Spicy Greens Soup

Serves 4-5

Ingredients

1 cup each kale, collards, and chard, chopped
4-5 cups water
2 tsp organic corn flour dissolved in 2 tbsp water
1 tsp cayenne pepper or 1 red hot chili pepper, chopped
2-3 tbsp ghee
1 tbsp fresh cilantro, chopped
½ tsp black pepper freshly ground
½ tsp sea salt or to taste
1 tsp nutritional yeast flakes (optional)

Instructions

Heat the ghee on medium heat in a large saucepan, add the chopped greens and chili (if using fresh) and sauté on low heat for 5-6 minutes. Add water and spices, including chili if using dry. Bring to boil on medium heat. Next, add the corn flour and simmer on low heat for

4-5 minutes. Remove from heat and add cilantro. Cover and let sit for five minutes. If using nutritional flakes, add them now.

Spicy Greens Soup II
Serves 4
Ingredients
1 cup each of kale and spinach, chopped
½ cup each of bok choy and mustard greens, chopped
4-5 cups water
2 tsp organic corn flour dissolved in 2 tbsp water
1 tbsp strong cayenne pepper or 3 red hot chili pepper, chopped
2-3 tbsp ghee
3 tbsp cilantro freshly, chopped
½ tsp black pepper freshly ground
1 tsp garlic, finely chopped or minced
1 tbsp ginger, finely chopped or minced
½ tsp Himalaya or sea salt or to taste
1 tsp nutritional yeast flakes (optional)
Instructions
Heat the ghee in a saucepan or large pot and add the chopped greens, garlic, ginger, and chili (if using fresh) and sauté on low heat for 5-6 minutes. Add the water and spices. Bring to boil on medium heat. Next, add the corn flour and simmer on low heat for 4-5 minutes. Remove from heat and add cilantro. Cover and let sit for 5 minutes. If using nutritional flakes, add now.

Vegetables

Lemon Pepper Broccoli
Serves 2-3
Ingredients
2 large broccoli crowns cut into florets
1 cup water

3-4 tbsp lemon juice
½ tsp fresh ground black pepper
½ tsp Himalaya or sea salt or 1 tbsp Braggs Liquid Amino Acids
2 tbsp ghee or coconut oil
1 tsp grated lemon peel
1 tbsp cilantro, finely chopped

Instructions

Boil or steam broccoli for 5-6 minutes. In a saucepan heat the ghee or coconut oil. Add broccoli, salt, pepper, and lemon, and sauté for 3-4 minutes. Remove from heat and mix in cilantro, cover and let sit for 5 minutes. Serve.

Awesome and Amazing Asparagus

Serves 2

Ingredients

2 cups asparagus stems, chopped
½ cup water
1 tsp lemon juice
1 tsp cumin powder
¼ tsp turmeric powder
¼ tsp paprika
¼ tsp black pepper
⅛ tsp coriander
¼ tsp Himalaya or sea salt
½ cup blanched, sliced almonds
2 tbsp ghee or coconut oil

Instructions

Heat the ghee on medium heat in a saucepan. Add the spices and sauté for a minute or two. Add asparagus and sauté for 3-4 minutes. Add water and cover. Cook until asparagus is tender (10-12 minutes). Stir frequently and add more water if necessary to prevent sticking. When the asparagus is finished, remove from heat and add lemon juice and almonds. Cover and let it sit for 5 minutes. Serve with dal or kichari.

Amazing Okra

Serves 2-3
Ingredients
2 tbsp ghee or coconut oil
3-4 green chilies, chopped
1 tbsp ginger, chopped into small pieces
4 large onions, chopped into small pieces
½ tsp turmeric powder
1½ lbs okra washed, dried, and cut into small strips lengthwise or into 5-6 rings per okra
¼ tsp black pepper
¼ tsp sea salt or to taste
¼ tsp basil
¼ tsp tarragon
Instructions
Heat the oil on medium heat in a saucepan and stir fry the green chilies and ginger slightly until the ginger turns a light brown. Add onions and stir fry on medium heat for 2-3 minutes or until onions are just about to brown. Stir in the turmeric. Add okra and other spices and cook briefly on high heat until it is well covered with oil and spices. Add salt and cook on low for 10-12 minutes or until okra is soft and well-cooked. Sauté for a few more minutes, until the okra is well done. Add a little more oil if necessary to avoid sticking. Cover and let sit for 5 minutes.

Broccoli and Peas Please! (Spicy)

Serves 2-3
Ingredients
1 onion, chopped into small pieces
2 cups broccoli, chopped into florets
1 cup green peas
2 tbsp ghee or coconut oil
a pinch of hing (asafoetida)
½ tsp turmeric powder

½ tsp cayenne pepper
½ tsp cumin powder
¼ tsp coriander powder
¼ tsp black pepper powder
⅛ tsp ginger powder
¼-½ tsp sea salt or to taste

Instructions

Steam or boil broccoli and peas until slightly soft. Heat ghee in a saucepan and sauté onions until they are just about to start browning. Add spices and sauté for a minute or two. Add broccoli and peas and sauté for 3-5 minutes. Add a little more ghee if necessary to avoid sticking. Cover and let sit for a few minutes.

Broccoli and Peas (Non-spicy Version)

Serves 2-3

Ingredients

1 onion, chopped into small pieces
2 cups broccoli, chopped into florets
1 cup green peas
2 tbsp ghee
a pinch of hing (asafoetida)
½ tsp rosemary
½ tsp basil
½ tsp dill
¼ tsp thyme
¼ tsp oregano
¼ cup cilantro, chopped
½ tsp Himalaya or sea salt

Instructions

Steam or boil broccoli and peas until slightly soft. Heat oil in a saucepan and sauté the onions until they are just about to start browning. Add spices and sauté for a minute or two. Add broccoli and peas and sauté for 3-5 minutes. Add a little more oil if necessary to avoid sticking. Cover and let sit for 5 minutes.

Beet and Spinach Save the Day

Serves 3-4
Ingredients
4 tbsp ghee or coconut oil
3 lbs spinach, chopped
2 cups beets, chopped
1 large onion, chopped
1 tbsp ginger freshly grated
⅛ tsp hing (asafoetida)
½ tsp turmeric
½ tsp cayenne pepper
1½ tsp Himalaya or sea salt
1 tsp cumin powder
½ tsp coriander powder
½ tsp black pepper
½ cup cilantro, chopped

Instructions

Heat the oil on medium heat in a large pan. Add beets, onions, and spinach. Stir-fry veggies for a couple of minutes. Add turmeric, cayenne pepper, and salt. Stir-fry until spinach is slightly soft. Add 2½ cups of water and the other spices. Cook on medium to medium-high for 10-12 minutes, stirring frequently, until just a little liquid is left and the beets are soft. Remove from heat and add cilantro. Cover and let sit 5 minutes.

Coconut Kale Extravaganza

Serves 2-3
Ingredients
3 cups kale, chopped
1 large garlic clove, crushed or finely chopped
3 whole large garlic cloves
1 tsp grated ginger
3 tbsp tamarind paste (available in Indian grocery stores or the international food section of most natural food stores)

⅛ tsp turmeric
½ tsp sea salt
½ tsp black pepper
¼ tsp cumin powder
¼ tsp cayenne pepper
3-4 tbsp ghee of coconut oil
3½ oz coconut milk
1 tbsp cilantro, chopped
¼ cup shredded coconut

Instructions

Place kale in a large mixing bowl. Add crushed garlic, ginger, tamarind paste, turmeric, salt, and cayenne pepper. Mix all together. Cover and let sit 15-20 minutes. Meanwhile, peel the 3 whole garlic cloves and crush. Heat oil on medium heat, add garlic, and stir until light golden brown. Add the kale mixture and stir-fry until cooked, about 5-7 minutes. Remove from heat and add coconut milk. Heat again and stir-fry until it starts to simmer, then remove from heat. Add cilantro and shredded coconut. Cover and let sit 7-10 minutes.

Coconut Vegetable Curry

Serves 4-5

Ingredients

1 cup broccoli florets
1 cup cauliflower florets
1 cup carrots, chopped into small pieces
1 cup green peas
1 large garlic clove, crushed
3 large garlic cloves
1 tbsp grated ginger
3 tbsp tamarind paste (available in Indian grocery stores or the international food section of most natural food stores)
⅛ tsp turmeric
½ tsp sea salt
½ tsp black pepper

½ tsp cumin powder
½ tsp coriander powder
¼ tsp cayenne pepper
3-4 tbsp coconut oil
4 oz (½ cup) coconut milk
2 tbsp cilantro, chopped into small pieces
2 medium sized green chili, chopped

Instructions

Boil or steam vegetables for 7-8 minutes. Keep the water. Peel the 3 whole garlic cloves and crush a little but keep whole as much as possible. Heat oil in a pan over medium flame. Add garlic and stir until light golden brown. Add vegetables and spices and stir-fry about 10 minutes, until almost cooked. Add a little of the vegetable water if necessary. Add coconut milk and green chilies. Stir-fry until it starts to simmer and remove from heat. Add cilantro, cover, and let sit for about 5 minutes.

Ghee Roast Root Vegetables

Serves 4-5

Ingredients

3 large parsnips, chopped
3 medium beets, chopped
2-8" burdock roots, chopped
3 carrots, chopped
4 tbsp ghee or coconut oil
⅛ tsp hing (asafoetida)
2 tsp black mustard seeds
1 tsp coriander powder
1 tsp cumin seeds
2 bay leaves
¼ tsp sea salt
½ tsp black pepper freshly ground
½ cup cilantro, chopped
½ cup water

Instructions

In a saucepan heat oil and cook all the herbs except cilantro for a couple of minutes. Add vegetables and sauté for another 3 minutes. Add water and cook for another 10-12 minutes. Remove from heat and add cilantro. Cover and let it sit for 10 minutes. Serve.

Herbal Beets

Serves 2-3

Ingredients

2 cups beets, cut into small pieces
1 cup yellow or red onions, chopped into small pieces
2 tsp garlic, minced
1 tbsp fresh basil, chopped
1 tsp dill
1 tsp oregano
4-5 threads of saffron
½ tsp black pepper freshly ground
¼ cu. Cilantro, chopped
2 tbsp ghee or coconut oil
½ tsp Himalaya or sea salt

Instructions

Boil or steam beets for 5 minutes. Heat oil, add spices and onions for 1-2 minutes. Add beets and spices, and sauté for about 5 minutes. Remove from heat and add salt and cilantro. Cover and let sit for 5 minutes. Add salt to taste. Serve.

Steamed Greens

Serves 4

Ingredients

2 cups collard greens, chopped
2 cups kale, chopped
2 cups mustard greens or chard, chopped
1 cup water
1 medium white or yellow onion, chopped into small pieces
½ tsp fresh ground black pepper

½ tsp sea salt
2 tbsp ghee or coconut oil
1 tsp fresh tarragon, chopped
1 tbsp dill
1 tbsp fresh basil, chopped
1 tbsp cilantro, chopped
¼-½ tsp cayenne pepper (optional)

Instructions

Steam greens for 4-5 minutes. In a saucepan heat the ghee and stir-fry onion for a few minutes until brown. Add greens, salt, pepper, and fresh herbs (except cilantro), and sauté for 2-3 minutes. If using cayenne pepper, add at this time. Remove from heat and mix in cilantro. Cover and let sit for 5 minutes. Serve.

Kale is Cool!

Serves 1-2

Ingredients

2 cups kale, chopped into small pieces
¼ tsp sea salt
¼ tsp black pepper powder
¼ tsp basil
¼ tsp dill
¼ tsp rosemary
1 tbsp ghee or coconut oil

Instructions

Steam kale for 5-6 minutes. Meanwhile, heat oil in a saucepan with spices (except salt) and sauté for about a minute. Add cooked kale and salt, and sauté for 2-3 minutes. Save the steamed kale water and if needed add a couple tablespoons to the sauté. Cover and let sit for a few minutes.

Options: Add 2-3 tbsp shredded coconut or ¼ cup chopped cilantro.

Simplicity Sesame Broccoli

Serves 3-4

Ingredients

4 cups broccoli florets

1 tsp ginger grated

½ tsp Himalaya or sea salt

2 tbsp organic toasted sesame oil

1 tbsp lemon juice

1-2 tbsp toasted sesame seeds

1 tsp black pepper powder

Instructions

Mix all ingredients (except broccoli) together in a bowl and let it sit. Steam broccoli for 4-5 minutes until slightly soft and remove from steamer. Add broccoli and sauce to a sauté pan. Cook for 3-4 more minutes. Remove from heat and cover. Let sit for 5-10 minutes. Serve.

Spicy Collards and Broccoli

Serves 3-4

Ingredients

2 cups broccoli, cut into florets

2 cups collard greens, chopped

1 cup water

1 small red onion, chopped into small pieces

3 or 4 hot chili peppers (or 1 heaping tsp cayenne pepper)

½ tsp fresh ground black pepper

½ tsp sea salt or to taste or 1 tbsp Braggs Liquid Amino Acids

2 tbsp ghee or coconut oil

1 tsp lemon peel, grated

1 tbsp cilantro, finely chopped

Instructions

Boil or steam broccoli and kale for 5-6 minutes. In a saucepan, heat oil and stir fry onion and chili for a few minutes until they start to brown. Mix in broccoli, kale, salt, and pepper and sauté for 2-3 minutes. If you are using cayenne pepper, add it at this time. Remove from heat, mix in cilantro, cover, and let sit for 5 minutes. Serve.

Steamed Garden Greens

Serves 2-3

Ingredients

1 cup kale

½ cup collard greens

½ cup bok choy

¼ cup arugula

¼ cup dandelion greens

¼ cup mustard greens

¼ cup chard

1 tsp dill

1 tsp basil

1 tbsp cilantro

½ tsp sea salt

½ tsp fine ground black pepper

Instructions

Chop greens. In a large stainless steel pot, boil 2 cups of water. Steam greens for 5 minutes and remove from heat. In a large bowl add greens, herbs, salt and pepper and mix thoroughly. Cover for a few minutes and let sit. Serve.

Part 2

Maintaining Health and Consciousness

14

The Doshas, Gunas, Ojas, Tejas, and Prana

In the cave of the body is eternally set the one unborn.

The earth is His body.
Though moving within the earth, the earth knows Him not.

The water is His body.
Though moving within the water, the water knows Him not.

The fire is His body.
Though moving within the fire, the fire knows Him not.

The air is His body.
Though moving within the air, the air knows Him not.

The ether is His body.
Though moving within the ether, the ether knows Him not.

The mind is His body.
Though moving within the mind, the mind knows Him not.

The intellect is His body.
Though moving within the intellect,
the intellect knows Him not.

The ego is His body.
Though moving within the ego, the ego knows Him not.

The mind-stuff is His body.
Though moving within the mind-stuff,
the mind-stuff knows Him not.

The unmanifest is His body.
Though moving within the unmanifest,
the unmanifest knows Him not.

The imperishable is His body.
Though moving within the imperishable,
the imperishable knows Him not.

The Death is His body.
Though moving within Death, Death knows Him not.

He, then, is the Inner-Self of all beings, sinless,
heaven-born, luminous, the Supreme Purusha.

~ Adhyatma Upanishad, Verse 1.1

The most fundamental and characteristic principle of Ayurveda is that of *tridosha,* or the three humors. All matter is composed of the five elements (*panchamahabhutas*) that exhibit the properties of earth (*prithvi*), water (*jala*), fire (*tejas*), wind (*vayu*), and space (*akasha*). The structural aspect of our body is made up of these five elements, but the functional aspect of the body is governed by three doshas. Ether and air constitute *vata*; fire, *pitta*; and water and earth, *kapha.* They govern psychobiological changes in the body and physio-pathological changes. Vata-pitta-kapha is present in every cell, tissue, and organ.

Doshas are to be seen as all-pervasive, subtle manifestations. Vata regulates movement and governs the nervous system. Pitta is the principle of biotransformation and governs the metabolic processes in the body. Kapha is the principle of cohesion and functions through the body fluids. In each individual, the three doshas manifest in different combinations and thereby determine the physiologic constitution (*prakriti*) of an individual. Vata, pitta, and kapha express differently in each human being.

All of creation is a dance or a play of these five elements. The word dosha actually means "vitiated" or out of balance. Such an imbalance occurs due to factors such as improper diet, seasonal changes, physical or mental stress, etc. Actually, the imbalance occurs to protect the body from physiological harm. In harmonious conditions, the doshas sustain balance within us. The doshas are responsible for biological, psychological and physio-pathological processes in our body, mind, and consciousness. They can maintain homeostasis or wreak havoc in our lives when they are disturbed.

Each individual in creation is a unique blend of the three doshas. From the three doshas come the seven constitutional types. There are the three mono dosha types—vata, pitta and kapha. There are three dual-dosha types—vata-pitta, vata-kapha, and pitta-kapha. Some people are *tridoshic*, meaning that they have an equal balance of all three (vata-pitta-kapha). When the tridoshas are balanced, the individual experiences health on all levels, mental, physical and spiritual.

When the following characteristics are in place, the doshas are said to be in balance, and a harmonious state of health is achieved.

1. Happiness—sense of well-being
2. Emotions—evenly balanced emotional states
3. Mental Functions—good memory, comprehension, intelligence, and reasoning ability
4. Senses—proper functioning of eyes, ears, nose, taste, and touch
5. Energy—abundant mental and physical energy
6. Digestion—easy digestion of food and drink
7. Elimination—normal elimination of wastes: sweat, urine, feces, and others
8. Physical Body—healthy bodily tissues, organs, and systems

There are generally two types of imbalances; natural and unnatural. Natural imbalances are due to time and age. Vata, pitta, and kapha increase and become predominant during one's life, during seasonal changes, and during certain times of day. For example, vata is predominant during the latter part of one's life, during the rainy season, and during late afternoon, as well as during the last part of night and the last part of digestion. Pitta is predominant during middle age, during the fall season, at midday, at midnight, and during the middle part of digestion. Kapha is predominant during childhood, during the spring season, in late morning, at the first part of evening, and during the early part of digestion. These natural imbalances can be rectified through lifestyle adjustments.

Imbalances of the doshas can be caused by inappropriate diet or lifestyle, physical, mental, or emotional trauma, viruses, parasites, etc. While some of these factors are beyond our control, the way we live, the foods we eat, and our actions are within our control. By following the correct lifestyle regime for our personal dosha we can minimize unnatural disturbances.

To learn to balance the doshas, one must first understand what causes each dosha to increase. According to the principles in Ayurveda, "Like increases like." For example, if you are cold and you eat ice cream, you will become colder. Herein lies one of the true beauties of Ayurveda: its principles are simple, basic, and natural.

Om Trikutayai Namah

I bow to Her who is in three parts.

~ Sri Lalita Sahasranama, verse 588

Vata

Vata is the energy of movement or prana that is part of everything in creation. Vata contains the ether and air elements, space, and movement. It is located in the thighs, hips, ears, bones, and the organs of hearing and touch, though its primary site is the colon. It governs assimilation and elimination. It is the impulse of expression, creativity, and propulsion. It gives life to all things.

Vata is responsible for breathing, movement, flexibility, and all biological processes. It governs the nervous system as well as our sensory and mental functions. Vata is dry, light, cold, mobile, active, clear, astringent, and dispersing. The rainy season is governed by vata. Vata times of day are afternoon and mid-to-late morning. In balance, vata has strong healing capabilities with robust energy and good health.

On a physical level, vata predominant individuals have thin, light, flexible bodies, often with protruding veins, tendons, and bones. They may also have small, recessed, and dry eyes. Their teeth are large and protruding with thin, small, dark, or chapped lips. They will have erratic appetite and thirst, which is one reason why their digestive systems are easily disturbed.

On an emotional and mental level, vatas are easily excited and act without considering what they are doing. They are very alert and aware but easily forget. They are quick and unsteady in thought, word, and actions. Often they are considered unreliable and indecisive. They tend to be fearful and lack courage due to high levels of anxiety.

A balanced vata is filled with light and love, has expansive consciousness, and sees the universal principle in all things. Additional indications of balanced vata are mental alertness and abundance of creative energy, good elimination of waste matters from the body, sound sleep, a strong immune system, enthusiasm, emotional balance, and orderly functioning of the body's systems. Signs of imbalanced vata are worry, fatigue, low stamina, nervousness, poor concentration, anxiety, fearfulness, agitation in the mind, impatience, feeling spacy, shyness, insecurity, restlessness, difficulty making decisions, being underweight, difficulty gaining weight, insomnia, waking up during the night, aching and painful body, swollen, stiff, and painful joints, sensitivity to cold, nail biting, rough, dry, and flaky skin, fainting, dizziness, heart palpitations, chapped lips, constipation, intestinal bloating, gas, belching, hiccups, dry eyes, and sore throat. These can be alleviated by following vata lifestyle regimes, which will be discussed in depth throughout this book. Vata dosha is further divided into five types according to its location and the different functions it performs.

Useful Tips to Balance Vata Dosha

To Balance Vata:
- *Abhyanga* (Ayurvedic oil massage)
- Stay warm in cold, windy weather.
- Consume predominately warm, cooked foods (less raw food).
- Go to bed early and have adequate rest and sleep.
- Favor warm, oily, heavy food with sweet, sour, and salty tastes.

Caution:
- Avoid light, dry, cold, pungent, bitter, and astringent foods.
- Avoid raw foods, juices, and fasting.
- Avoid stimulants, smoking, and alcohol.
- Refrain from excessive aerobic activity.

Pitta

Pitta is fiery and transformative. It gives light and energy. Pitta is the seat of our digestive fire. The word pitta comes from the root *tapa,* which means heat. This dosha is responsible for digestion and metabolism. Pitta is located in the small intestines, stomach, sweat and sebaceous glands, blood, lymph, and eyes. It rules over blood and nourishment. Pitta is hot, moist, light, subtle, mobile, sharp, soft, smooth, and clear. It is governed by tejas, that which brings forth the inner light of consciousness. Pitta is responsible for all transformation in our body and mind. It gives one the perception to comprehend reality and understand the true nature of things.

Pitta-predominant people can be highly sensitive and react easily without much provocation. They tend toward anger and rage when disturbed. They have the ability to be great leaders and have strong intellectual capabilities. A pitta person has a medium build with solid muscle tone and a bright complexion. Their eyes are piercing, and their lips are soft and often found smiling. They tend to bald early in life, often due to excessive heat in the body or mind. They have a strong appetite for food and life that can drive them into excess. Pittas do best in cool, calm environments that balance their internal fire.

When a person exhibits strong powers of digestion, vitality, goal-setting inclinations, good problem-solving skills, keen powers of intelligence, decisiveness, boldness, courage, and a bright complexion, pitta is balanced.

Pitta is imbalanced when there is excessive body heat, digestive problems, hostility or anger, a tendency to be overly controlling and impatient, exertion of excessive effort to achieve goals, vision difficulties, a tendency to make errors in judgment due to mental confusion, and passion or emotions that distort one's power of discernment.

Useful Tips to Balance Pitta Dosha

To Balance Pitta:
- Keep cool. Avoid hot temperatures.
- Favor cool, heavy, dry, sweet, bitter, and astringent foods.
- Keep activities in moderation.
- Keep regular mealtimes, especially lunchtime.

Caution:
- Avoid sesame and mustard oils, fish, buttermilk, acidic fruits, alcohol, meat, and fatty, oily foods.
- Restrict pungent, sour, salty, warm, oily, and light foods.
- Avoid overworking.
- Avoid excessive or prolonged fasting.

Kapha

Kapha is governed by water and earth. It binds things together and solidifies creation. Kapha is also called *slesma* (slimy/sticky). One of its main functions is to provide nutrition to bodily tissues. Kapha is nourishment and support. It is located in the chest, throat, head, pancreas, sides, stomach, fat, nose, and tongue. Kapha creates bodily tissues and holds the bones and muscles together. Kapha, like Mother Earth, is abundant and giving. Kapha-predominant types are motherly, patient, and compassionate. They have energy to endure through long and arduous tasks. They tend to be slow learners but once they have learned something, they never forget it. They are pure and gentle, yet firm.

Kapha is heavy, slow, cold, oily, wet/liquid, slimy, dense, soft, static, sticky, cloudy, and gross. Kapha bodily frames are large with large eyes, lips, and bones, and with thick skin and strong teeth. Their hair is full and often curvy or very wavy. They have a consistent appetite with slow to sluggish digestion. They have deep faith in God and love for humanity. Kapha types are abundant with health, fertility, and longevity. However, when out of balance, they are "couch potatoes." Kaphas tend to be overweight and can become obese. They can become lifeless or lazy. Their minds become dull and move into slumps of depression and non-responsiveness, becoming almost catatonic. When kapha is harmonized, it has excellent strength, knowledge, peace, contentment, love, and longevity. In India, kapha is often considered to be the most desirable constitution. (Whereas in the West, vata is preferred, as is reflected in most of the advertising, modeling, and popular diet programs.)

Kapha is balanced when there is physical strength, a strong immune system, serenity, mental resolve, rational thinking, endurance, adaptability, love, compassion, and an ability to conserve and use personal resources.

Imbalances in kapha are indicated by sluggish thinking, grogginess, apathy, loss of desire, depression, sadness, sentimentality, slow comprehension, slow reaction, procrastination, lethargy, clinginess, greedy, possessiveness, materialism, sleeping too much, exhaustion in the morning, drowsiness during the day, weight gain, obesity, congestion in the chest or throat, mucus and congestion of the sinuses, nausea, diabetes, hay fever, skin that is pale, cool, and clammy, edema, bloated feeling, sluggish digestion, high cholesterol, and aching joints or heavy limbs. These kapha excesses can be diminished by following kapha lifestyle regimes.

Useful Tips to Balance Kapha Dosha
To Balance Kapha:
Exercise regularly. Begin with Surya Namaskar (sun salutations) to warm up the body, which should be followed by vigorous activity.
Prefer warm temperatures. Stay warm and dry in cold, damp weather.
Eat fresh fruits, vegetables, and legumes.
Favor pungent, bitter, astringent, light, dry, and warm foods.
Caution:
Reduce heavy, oily, cold, sweet, sour, and salty foods.
Avoid heavy meals.
Sleep promotes kapha, hence avoid excessive sleep.
All frozen desserts are to be avoided.
Determining one's dosha and following the appropriate lifestyle modifications is essential for living a harmonious, disease-free life. Dietary and lifestyle regimes vary depending on the unique balance of the individual.

The Three Gunas

Om Trigunayai Namah

*I bow to Her who is endowed with the three
gunas of sattva, rajas, and tamas.*

~ Sri Lalita Sahasranama, verse 984

The *gunas* are the manifested aspects, or the primary original qualities of the doshas. These are the three qualities of the mind that are
interconnected with the three vital forces of the body. The mental
nature of a person can be categorized according to the gunas, the
primary attributes of nature: sattvic (pure or essence), rajasic (movement), and tamasic (inertia). Just as the doshas are the essential components of the body, the three gunas—sattva, rajas, and tamas—are
the three essential components or energies of the mind. The three
gunas are found in nature as well, paralleling the three doshas of
the body. Ayurveda offers a clear description of people on the basis
of their psychological constitution *(manas prakriti)*. All individuals
have a combined union of the three, wherein the predominant guna
determines an individual's mental nature.

In balance, the three gunas maintain a healthy state of mind
(and to some extent, of body as well). The three gunas are the very
fabric of creation as they permeate through all living and non-living,
tangible and intangible things. An object's predominant guna determines the vibrations it emits and its behavior. Disturbances to the
harmony of the gunas result in different types of mental disorders.
The development of a *sattvic* mind is a goal of yoga and Ayurveda.

The three gunas manifest in our bodies, mind, and consciousness. Although they are more subtle than the doshas, disturbances
in the gunas create disturbances in the gross body. The gunas make
up our mental disposition and spiritual inclinations. Everyone has
sattva, rajas, and tamas within them, in some proportion. The key
is to keep them balanced and in harmony with each other and with
the *manas prakriti*.

Sattva

Om Maha-Sattvayai Namah

I bow to She who possesses great sattva.

~ Sri Lalita Sahasranama, Verse 216

Often considered to be the pure state of mind or consciousness, sattva is a clear, light, innocent, and undisturbed inner state of being. It is content and divine in nature. Sattva is the union of the heart and mind. It is virtuous, patient, and compassionate.

A sattvic mind reflects clarity of perception and peace of mind. One endowed with a sattvic nature is free from suffering and is a beacon of light for the world. Sattvic types are always engaged in good actions, and work toward the betterment of humanity.

As we increase the amount of the sattva guna within us, our spiritual vibration and the positive aspects of our personalities are greatly enhanced. One who is endowed with sattva will have control over emotions, thoughts, and actions. They will possess all virtues, and will adhere to dharma. They will be lawful, tolerant, and serene. They will possess a stable intellect and not be egotistical. A sattvic person is a living example to the world, serving society and assisting others to grow spiritually by increasing their awareness and compassion.

The mind (manas) as well as the *pancha jnanendriyas* (five sensory organs), and the *pancha karmendriyas* (five organs of actions) manifest from the union of sattva and rajas.

Rajas

Om Manomayyai Namah

I bow to She who is in the pure form of the mind.

~ Sri Lalita Sahasranama, Verse 941

Rajas is the nature of movement or action. It has the power of observation. Rajas is the active force that moves sattva into action. With rajas present, the pure mind is disturbed, agitated, or active. The mind's gaze is now looking outward. When we look outward, we start desiring; thus, rajas is the essence of desire. The most active of the gunas, rajas characterizes motion and stimulation. All desires and aspirations are a result of rajas. It influences all its endeavors, including the logical, rational, and thinking mind, creating indecisiveness, unreliability, hyperactivity, and anxiety. Rajas creates lust and greed for money, material luxuries, and comfort. When one has desire, attachment follows. These attachments are the cause of all suffering. Rajas can become self-serving, considering only its interest at any cost. When desires are not fulfilled, more suffering results.

Rajas, when balanced with sattva, manifests love and compassion. When disturbed it brings anger, rage, hostility, and disease. Rajas is the manifestation of ego or individualization. The five organs of action (mouth, hands, feet, reproductive organs, and eliminatory organs) come from rajas. Mind is also the active principle of rajas.

Tamas

Om Tamopahayai Namah

I bow to She who removes the ignorance of tamas.

~ Sri Lalita Sahasranama, Verse 361

Tamas is the nature of destruction or dissolution. It is darkness. Tamas is the inability to perceive light or consciousness. Excess tamas is inertia. Tamas is characterized by heaviness and resistance. Delusion, laziness, apathy, and drowsiness are due to it. Sedative in nature, tamas causes pain and suffering, and leads one toward depression.

Tamas manifests as blocked emotions. It is the nature of destruction, degeneration, and death. Tamas is unfulfilled desire suppressed in the recesses of the subconscious mind. The presence of tamas creates vindictiveness, violence, hate, criminality, and psychopathic behavior. Its nature is animalistic, delusional, self-serving, materialistic, and demonic. Tamas rules over the earth and the five elements as it contains all the doshas. The goal of yoga is to balance and control tamas, rajas, and sattva within one's consciousness, resulting in an awakening of the Divine within.

The three doshas are the gross manifestation of the three gunas. The three *doshas* are governed by the twenty attributes or qualities of Nature (*prakriti*), which manifest as ten pairs of opposites and are the dual forces of the universe.

The 10 pairs of opposites

- cold/hot (*shita/ushna*)
- oily or wet/dry *(snigha/ruksha)*
- heavy/light *(guru/laghu)*
- gross/subtle *(sthula/sukshma)*
- dense/liquid *(sandra/drava)*
- stable/mobile *(sthira/chala)*
- slow or dull/sharp *(mandha/tikshna)*
- soft/hard *(mridu/kathina)*
- slimy or smooth/rough *(slakshna/khara)*
- clear/cloudy *(vishada/pichilla)*

Twenty attributes that relate directly to the doshas

- **Hot** relates to pitta and the fire element. It increases pitta while decreasing vata and kapha.
- **Cold** relates to kapha and vata and increases both, while decreasing pitta.
- **Dry** is one of the primary attributes of vata. Dryness greatly increases vata, yet greatly decreases kapha and mildly decreases pitta.
- **Wet** is the primary attribute of kapha dosha and the water element. It increases kapha, decreases vata and mildly increases pitta.
- **Heavy** correlates to the earth and water element, thus it increases kapha. It decreases both vata and pitta (moderately).

- **Light** is of the fire, space, and air elements so it greatly increases vata, moderately increases pitta, and decreases kapha.
- **Gross** is similar in qualities to heavy as it relates to earth and water. It increases kapha and decreases vata and pitta.
- **Subtle** is similar to light. It increases vata and pitta while decreasing kapha.
- **Dense** also relates to earth. It increases kapha and decreases vata and pitta.
- **Liquid** or **flowing** corresponds to water and fire. It increases pitta and decreases vata and kapha.
- **Mobile** relates primarily to air, but also to fire. It greatly increases vata and moderately pitta. It decreases kapha.
- **Stable**, or sometimes called **static** or **slow**, relates to water and earth elements. It increases kapha and decreases vata and pitta.
- **Dull** corresponds to earth and water. It increases kapha and decreases vata and pitta.
- **Sharp** relates to fire, space/ether, and air. It increases pitta and vata while decreasing kapha.
- **Soft** corresponds to water. It increases kapha while decreasing pitta and vata.
- **Hard** relates to the earth and air elements. It increases vata while decreasing pitta and kapha.
- **Smooth** is similar to soft. It relates primarily to water. It greatly increases kapha and mildly increases pitta. It decreases vata.
- **Rough** is of the earth and air elements. It increases vata and decreases pitta and kapha.
- **Clear** or **light** corresponds to fire, ether, and air. It increases vata and pitta while decreasing kapha.
- **Dark** or **cloudy** is of the earth and water elements. It increases kapha and decreases pitta and vata.

Other qualities such as masculine and feminine are also present in the doshas. Pitta is more masculine while kapha is feminine. Vata is neutral. The balance of the masculine and feminine energies within oneself depends on the *prakriti*. It is ideal to have equal amounts of both masculine and feminine energies.

Ojas, Tejas, Prana

The mind alone is the cause of bondage and liberation.
The mind that is attached to the objects of the senses
leads them to bondage.
Freed from the objects of attachment,
it leads them to liberation.

~ Satyayaniya Upanishad, Verse 1.1

The doshas are composed of the five elements. Ojas, tejas, and prana are the very subtle forms of the doshas. These three are the positive, life-giving aspects of the doshas. Prana is our vital life force and is the healing energy of vata. Tejas is our inner light and is the healing energy of pitta. Ojas is the ultimate energy reserve of the body that manifests from kapha. In Ayurveda, one desires to reduce excess in the doshas to prevent disease while developing more prana, tejas, and ojas for good health. One with strong, healthy prana has vitality, breath, circulation, movement, and adaptability. One endowed with good tejas has radiance, luster in the eyes, clarity, insight, courage, compassion, and fearlessness. A person with strong ojas has strong immunity, endurance, calmness, and contentment.

The most crucial factor we want to develop is ojas, the higher aspect of kapha dosha. Ojas is the essential root power, our basic energy. Ideally, one will have a harmonious balance of all three. Like the doshas and gunas it is necessary that these elements are in unison with each other and within our consciousness, giving us physical, psychological, and spiritual stamina.

Ojas in its pure subtle form relates to kapha and the water element. Tejas in its subtle form relates to pitta and the fire element. Prana in its subtle form relates to vata and the ether element. They are often compared to the principles of *yin, yang,* and *chi* of the Chinese medical system, with ojas being the yin; tejas, the yang; and prana, the chi. When ojas, tejas, and prana function harmoniously, the mind enters a state of waking stillness and we experience the natural state peace deep within our Self. As with the doshas, when our life force is out of balance, we feel disturbed and our health diminishes. If we maintain balance, then our life becomes peaceful and happy and free from disease.

Ojas

Om Prema-Rupayai Namah

I bow to Her who is Pure Love.

~ *Sri Lalita Sahasranama, Verse 730*

Ojas is the accumulated vital reserve, the basis of physical and mental energy. Ojas is the internalized essence of digested food, water, air, impressions, and thoughts. On an inner level it is responsible for nourishing and developing all higher facilities. Ojas is our core vitality. It is the basic capacity of the immune system to defend our bodies against external pathogens. Ojas provides endurance, resistance, and strength to ward off diseases. It affords not only physical immunity, but emotional and mental immunity as well. It is a superfine substance that gives strength to the bodily tissues, organs, and processes.

Ojas is the motherly qualities of nurturance and love. Without ojas, we are lifeless. Ojas is the pure vibration of love and compassion in the heart. When one is filled with love, the gross and subtle immune system is very strong and disease cannot penetrate into the body. Ojas is the product of pure thoughts and actions as well as the intake of pure foods and impressions. It gives us mental strength, contentment, purity, patience, calmness, adaptability, and excellent mental faculties. Ojas is also the auric field that, when strong, emits a beautiful, serene glow of golden light. This field protects us from external negative influences.

Ojas is increased and maintained through proper diet (sattvic, vegetarian, or vegan), tonic herbs, sensory control (including celibacy or proper use of sexual energy), and bhakti yoga (including *seva* or selfless service).

Foods that increase ojas are whole grains, fruits and vegetables (especially root vegetables), nuts and seeds, pure quality dairy (not pasteurized or homogenized), pure water, and air. Dates, almonds, and ghee are especially beneficial ojas-increasing foods and can be taken together as a tonic.

Tejas

Om Parasmai Jyotise Namah

I bow to Her who is the Supreme Light.

~ Sri Lalita Sahasranama, Verse 806

Tejas is our inner light and the subtle energy of the fire element, pitta. It is the radiant mental vitality through which we digest our air, impressions, and thoughts. On an inner level, it unfolds our higher perceptual abilities. Tejas is the fire of intellect, knowledge, and reason. It gives the power of proper discrimination such as knowing the eternal from the non-eternal, and right from wrong. Tejas is the power of *sadhana* or spiritual practices, such as self-discipline, scriptural study, and mantra japa. Tejas is necessary for *jnana yoga*, the yoga of knowledge. It bestows clarity of mind and speech, as well as courage and faith. It gives the power to know the Self and the endurance to persist on the path towards the One. Practices like *atma-vicharya* (Self-inquiry) increase the intensity of tejas within the mind and heart.

Like ojas, tejas is a vital part of our immunity. Tejas is the immune system's ability to burn and destroy toxins. When activated, it generates fever to destroy pathogens that attack the body. Tejas is our ability to attack and overcome acute diseases, which are generally infectious in nature. As fire, it is the power of digestion and trans-formation of our food, thoughts, emotions, and actions. Someone with strong tejas will have bright, penetrating eyes, lustrous skin, and an attractive personality.

Tejas can be increased and maintained by performing *tapas* (purification by heat or spiritual practices), such as controlling the tongue (fasting and observing silence). It is often said that if we cannot control the tongue we will never be able to control the mind. Chanting of mantras is an excellent way to harness the pure quality of the tongue and the mind. Studying scriptures is also very beneficial. One must do spiritual practices under the guidance of a competent guide so as to protect tejas from becoming too high. If tejas becomes too high it can end up depleting ojas and harming the nervous system.

Prana

Om Prana-Datryai Namah

I bow to Her who is the giver of life.

~ Sri Lalita Sahasranama, Verse 832

Prana is our vital life force and the subtle energy of the air ele-ment, vata. As the divine force and guiding intelligence behind all psycho-physical functions, it is responsible for coordination of breath, senses, and mind. On an inner level, it awakens and balances all higher states of consciousness. Prana governs all aspects of our lives, physical and spiritual. Prana is our ability of coordination and speech. Prana is the essence of sound and it governs all mantras. It is the breath that gives life; it literally breathes life into all creation. It is our creative impulse and desire for evolution. It is the pull of the unmanifest calling us home. Prana unifies *Shiva* and *Shakti* (*purusha*

151

and *prakriti*). It is the *Kundalini Shakti* lying dormant at the base of the spine waiting to merge with Her beloved in the crown of our head at the lotus of infinite brilliant light, the Self.

Prana is the vitalized activation of the immune system's natural function to project and develop our life force. It manifests when we are fighting off chronic diseases. It is the adaptability of the immune system and sustains all long-term healing processes. With sufficient prana, tejas, and ojas, no disease can harm us.

Prana is increased through practices like meditation, pranayama, Hatha Yoga, and the chanting of mantras, especially om. Prana is the unifying factor between ojas and tejas. Once ojas is present, tejas is born. Prana develops from the union of ojas and tejas. Ojas and tejas could not sustain themselves without prana.

Prana, tejas, and ojas are the divine manifestations of the three doshas. According to Ayurveda, when the doshas are too high or too low, they cause disease. But prana, tejas, and ojas, unlike the doshas, promote health, creativity, and well-being, and provide support for deeper sadhana. Prana, tejas, and ojas do not cause disease. They are the radiant manifestations in our life. We only have disease if they are lacking. As with all things in creation, conditions of excess and deficiency can arise when prana, tejas, and ojas are out of balance.

Prana in excess creates a loss of mental control, and sense and motor function. Its predominant manifestation is a lack of grounding or centering within one's own self. Deficient prana causes mental dullness or a lack of mental energy, enthusiasm, and creativity.

Tejas in excess causes the mind to become very critical and discriminating. Emotional outbursts of anger, irritation, and rage may follow. There will often be headaches, fever, and burning sensations in the head or eyes. When tejas is weak there will be a passiveness, a lack of proper discrimination, and an inability to learn from life. Motivating factors fall away from life and result in a lack of courage and ambition.

Ojas in excess may cause sluggishness of the mental faculties. An imbalanced self-contentment may lead to lack of desire to progress on one's spiritual path. An excess of ojas may manifest as high cholesterol or high kapha. A deficiency of ojas is very common due to excess use of stimulants, sex, external input, and a drive toward overindulgence. Weak ojas appears as a lack of concentration, poor memory, low self-esteem, a lack of faith and devotion, diminished or no motivation, nervous exhaustion, and immune weakness.

Prana, tejas, and ojas may be increased through not only spiritual practices, but also positive impressions such as positive life experiences, right diet, walks in nature, warm baths, and use of colors, gemstones, crystals, and essential oils. Spending time in nature most effectively increases prana. Sitting, walking or doing spiritual practices near fresh bodies of water or in a secluded forest all increase prana, tejas, and ojas tremendously, as nature is the true healer.

Diet, Doshas, and Gunas

Both Ayurveda and yoga emphasize "right diet" as the foundation of all healing therapies. Food is the first and most important form of medicine. A famous Ayurvedic saying expounds, "If right diet is followed, no medicines are necessary. If wrong diet is followed, no medicines can help." Ayurveda and yoga recommend a sattvic or pure food diet (following *ahimsa,* non-harm), as it creates balance and eliminates harmful factors (physical and vibrational), while reducing excesses in the doshas. In ancient times everything was believed to have a medicinal benefit. It is strongly encouraged to follow a purely vegetarian diet.

In the present day, eating animals has numerous health, environmental, political, and socio-economic consequences. Scientific research shows that animal meat, fat, proteins, and cholesterol promote cancer, heart disease, diabetes, obesity, and numerous other diseases. A vegetarian diet follows the principles of ahimsa and sattva, avoiding any products that involve killing of animals. In most scenarios eating the flesh of an animal violates the principles of ahimsa. Eating pure, organic food supports good health, as non-organic food is produced using violent and destructive farming practices that harm the Earth, our Mother. This subject will be discussed in detail later in the book.

Most humans cannot readily break down animal tissues into the proper nutrients for human tissues. Instead of digesting and transforming meat into the appropriate human tissue, the animalistic energies are preserved and become part of our human tissues. Thus, eating animals increases the animalistic tendencies in our bodies and brings the traits of the animal to live within us, promoting anger, lust, fear, and other negative emotions. Dead animals produce a heavy or tamasic type of tissue that clogs the channels *(nadis)*, making the mind dull and lethargic. On an economic level, the grain used to produce meat to serve one family could easily serve five or more families. The entire economic and environmental status of the world would change if most people resolved to become vegetarians.

Bhuta maintmanay - kali
porikalaintumanay
bodhamaki nintray - kali
poriyai vinci nintray

You became the five elements, Kali,
and you became the five senses.
You became awareness, Kali,
and you became the spirit.

~ Yadumaki Nintray (Tamil)

15

The Ayurvedic Diet: Food as Medicine

The Ayurvedic physician begins the cure of disease by arranging the diet that is to be followed by the patient. The Ayurvedic physicians rely so much on diet that it is declared that all diseases can be cured by following dietetic rules carefully along with the proper herbal supplements; but if a patient does not attend to his diet, a hundred good medicines will not cure him.

~ Charaka Samhita, 1.41

The Ayurvedic diet not only nourishes the body, but also restores the balance of the doshas, which is essential for maintaining health. An Ayurvedic diet is based on an individual's constitution. Medicine for one person may be poison for another. Each individual has unique dietary requirements; depending on one's dosha, or constitutional type, some foods can be beneficial and others should be avoided. When choosing what to eat, one must consider the season, weather, time of day, and quality of food, as well as one's mental and emotional attitudes at the time of eating.

When we ingest food, we participate in the creative process of Nature. Healthful food rejuvenates the cells of the body, especially our stomach lining and skin. How we eat also determines how food affects our body. If we feel emotionally imbalanced when we eat, our food may disrupt the body's natural order. If we overeat or eat too quickly, the poorly digested end product predisposes us to ill health.

Food intake should contribute to order and coherence in the body. It should help us to stay balanced and boost our overall immunity.

Every food contains the five elements and the three doshas in different proportions. Consumption of each food will affect our elemental doshic balance in a positive or a negative way. If a person already has an element in sufficient quantity by inheritance, he or she should be careful not to ingest too much of that element, or an imbalance may manifest. Following an Ayurvedic diet is not difficult. For every food that will aggravate the doshas, there are plenty of alternative, beneficial and tasty foods. Wrong eating habits are a result of past conditioning by family, friends, and society. By creating new dietary patterns, we can enhance all the levels of our well-being.

The following are general principles that should be followed when eating. They will assure optimum digestion, assimilation, and elimination. Never overeat. Half the stomach should be for food, a quarter for liquid, and the remaining portion for the movement of air. The less food you eat, the more mental control you will have. Do not sleep or meditate immediately after eating; if you do, you won't be able to digest the food properly. Always mentally repeat your mantra while you eat. This will purify the food and your mind at the same time.

~ Amma

- Eat to about three-quarters of your capacity. Do not leave the table very hungry or very full.
- Avoid taking a meal until the previous meal has been digested. Allow approximately 3-6 hours between meals.
- Eat in a settled and quiet atmosphere. Do not work, read, or watch TV during meal times. Avoid talking, if possible.
- Choose foods by balancing physical attributes. In general, the diet should be balanced to include all six tastes. Follow specific recommendations according to your constitution. In Ayurveda, foods are classified into six tastes: sweet, sour, salty,

bitter, pungent, and astringent. Ayurvedic practitioners recommend including all of these six tastes in every meal. Each taste has a balancing effect, so including some of each minimizes cravings and balances the appetite and digestion. The general North American and European diet tends to have too much of the sweet, sour, and salty tastes, and not enough of the bitter, pungent, and astringent tastes.

- Choose foods that are sattvic. Namely, whole, fresh, in-season, local foods.
- Yogurt, cheese, cottage cheese, and buttermilk should be avoided at night.
- Follow food-combining guidelines (listed later in the book).
- It is best not to cook with honey as it becomes poison (*visha*) and toxic (ama) when cooked.
- Take a few minutes to sit quietly after a meal before returning to activity.
- Follow proper eating rules: have breakfast at 7-9 a.m., lunch at 10-2 p.m., and dinner at 4-6 p.m.
- Wash face, hands, and feet before meals. Dine in an isolated, neat, and clean place. The environment should be pleasant. The eater should be in a comfortable seated position.
- Eat only food prepared by loving hands in a loving way. This method of food preparation increases the vitality-giving quality of the food.
- Chew food until it is an even consistency before swallowing.
- Hard items should be consumed in the beginning of the meal, followed by soft foods, and subsequently, liquids.
- Do not consume cold drinks just prior to or while eating. Also, do not drink large quantities of liquids during meals. This habit weakens digestion. A few sips of warm water is okay with meals.
- Heavy substances such as rich desserts after meals should be avoided.
- Consumption of excessively hot food leads to weakness. Cold and dry foods lead to delayed digestion.

- No travel or vigorous exercise or sexual intercourse within one hour after a meal, as this will impede digestion. Walking after a meal for 15-30 minutes can help digestion.
- Avoid meals when thirsty and water when hungry.
- Avoid meals immediately after exertion.
- Avoid meals when there is not an appetite.
- Don't suppress the appetite, as this leads to body pain, anorexia, lassitude, vertigo, and general debility.
- Don't suppress thirst, as it leads to general debility, giddiness, and heart disease.

Eating Habits That Decrease Health

- Overeating
- Eating when not hungry
- Emotional eating
- Drinking juice or excess water while eating
- Drinking chilled water at any time
- Eating when constipated or emotionally imbalanced
- Eating at the wrong time of day
- Eating too many heavy foods or not enough light foods
- Snacking on anything except fruit in between meals
- Eating incompatible food combinations

Six Types of Nutritional Imbalances

1. Quantitative Deficiency: malnutrition due to insufficient food
2. Quantitative Excess: excessive amounts of any food or water, food taken at the wrong time, and food not appropriate for constitution
3. Qualitative Deficiency: wrong food-combining, which results in malnutrition, toxic conditions, and lack of essential nutrients
4. Qualitative Excess: emotional overeating; eating foods that are fried, rich or high in fat, wrong foods for constitution

5. Ama Producing: eating foods and improper food-combinations that lead to toxemia and other digestive disorders; this includes eating foods with toxins such as pesticides, herbicides, hormones, and antibiotics

6. Prakriti Disturbing: eating foods not appropriate for one's constitution, which may lead to reduced agni and immunity, resulting in disease

These six factors lead to depletion of *agni* and the buildup of *ama* (toxins).

Benefits of a Sattvic Diet

The person who always eats wholesome (sattvic) food,
enjoys a regular lifestyle,
remains unattached to the objects of the senses,
gives and forgives,
loves truth, and serves others without disease.

~ Ashtanga Hridayam

When food is pure, the mind is pure; this creates an
oasis for awakening and provides an awakening that
affects every level of our health [body-mind-spirit].

~ Chandogya Upanishad

Ayurveda encourages eating a sattvic diet. The rishis gave criteria for eating a sattvic diet. It includes:

1. Foods grown in healthy fertile soil

2. Foods that are attractive in appearance (ripe and bountiful)

3. Foods that are protected from animals (insects, parasites, worms, and harmful bacteria)

Modern Day Additions:

1. Food should be grown without pesticides, herbicides, fungicides, chemical fertilizers, hormones, antibiotics, irradiation, GMOs, etc. This includes not harming the earth or its inhabitants (ahimsa).

2. Food should be whole, fresh, and unprocessed/unrefined, rather than canned, preserved, etc., with no chemical additives.

3. Animal food is dead; it is tamasic and there is no life force. Sattvic food contains between 75-90% water content. It is filled with prana and nourishes life.

Sattvic foods prevent free radicals because they are rich in antioxidants. Free radicals destroy enzymes and amino acids, and block cellular function. Free radicals are electron-deficient molecules that are produced from oxygen and heated fats or oils in the body. They destroy health. Health and longevity are dependent on hydration and antioxidant-rich foods.

Food-Combining Guidelines

Don't eat these foods	With these foods
Beans	Fruit, cheese, eggs, fish, milk, meat, yogurt
Eggs	Milk, fruit, beans, cheese, fish, kichari, meat, yogurt
Grains	Fruit
Fruit	Any other food, except dates/almonds are okay

Honey	Honey & ghee by equal weight: avoid 1 teaspoon honey/3 teaspoon ghee (1 teaspoon each is okay). Ayurveda recommends that honey should not be cooked. When cooked, honey becomes sticky glue that adheres to mucous membranes and clogs the gross and subtle channels, producing toxins. Raw honey is considered to be *amrita* (nectar).
Hot Drinks	Mangoes, cheese, fish, meat, starch, yogurt
Lemon	Cucumbers, milk, tomatoes, yogurt
Melons	Any other food, including other melons
Milk	Fruit especially bananas, cherries, melons, and sour fruit, bread, fish, kichari, meat. Ayurveda also finds that pasteurized and/or homogenized dairy causes ama, and is not recommended. Additionally, Ayurveda recommends consuming raw dairy, and avoiding dairy produced in factory farms that use hormones, antibiotics, and steroids.
Nightshades (tomato, eggplant, bell pepper, potato)	Cucumber, dairy products
Radishes	Bananas, raisins, milk
Tapioca/ Yogurt	Milk, fruit, cheese, eggs, fish, hot drinks, meat, nightshades

The Six Tastes

The six tastes are based on the actual taste in the mouth. Each taste has unique therapeutic properties. This applies to food, herbs, and minerals. Balancing the tastes according to dosha is the key to health. Each of the tastes is governed by two of the five elements, and either increases or decreases the doshas.

1. **Sweet:** made of earth and water; decreases vata and pitta, increases kapha
   - Sweet fruits: figs, grapes, oranges, dates, pears
   - Most legumes: beans, lentils, peas
   - Most grains: wheat, rice, corn, barley, most bread
   - Milk and sweet milk products: cream, ghee, butter
   - Sugar and sweeteners: white and refined sugars, artificial sweeteners, jaggery, maple syrup; honey, having a secondary taste of astringent, decreases vata and kapha, and increases pitta
   - Certain cooked vegetables: starchy tubers like potato, carrot, sweet potato, beet root

2. **Sour:** made of earth and fire; decreases vata, increases pitta and kapha
   - Sour milk products: yogurt, cheese, whey, sour cream
   - Sour fruits: lemon, sour orange, etc.
   - Fermented substances: soy sauce, vinegar, wine, sour cabbage (kimchi), pickles

3. **Salty:** made of water and fire; decreases vata, increases pitta and kapha
   - Salt: sea salt, Himalaya salt, rock salt, table salt, soy sauce, tamari, any other form of salt
   - Salty food: seaweed, salty pickles, chips

4. **Pungent:** made of fire and air; decreases kapha, increases pitta and vata
   - Vegetables: radish, onion, garlic
   - Spices: ginger, cumin, garlic, chili, mustard seeds, black pepper, hing

5. **Bitter:** made of air and ether; decreases pitta and kapha, increases vata
   - Fruits: olives, grapefruit
   - Vegetables: eggplant, chicory, bitter gourd
   - Green leafy vegetables: spinach, green cabbage, Brussels sprouts, zucchini

- Spices: fenugreek, turmeric, coriander
6. **Astringent:** made of air and earth; increases vata, decreases pitta and kapha
   - Sweetener: honey decreases vata and kapha while increasing pitta due to its heating properties
   - Nuts: walnuts, hazelnuts
   - Legumes: beans, lentils
   - Vegetables: sprouts, lettuce, rhubarb, green leafy vegetables, most raw vegetables
   - Fruits: persimmons, cashews, berries, pomegranates, unripe fruits, and to some degree, apples

Vata is decreased by sweet, sour, and salty tastes. It is also decreased by foods that are heavy, oily, and hot. Vata is increased by pungent, bitter, and astringent tastes, as well as foods that are light, dry, and cold.

Pitta is decreased by sweet, bitter, and astringent tastes, and cold, heavy, and oily foods. Pitta is increased by pungent, sour, and salty tastes as well as foods that are hot, light, and dry.

Kapha is decreased by pungent, bitter, and astringent tastes in foods that are light, dry, and warm. Kapha is increased by sweet, sour, and salty tastes, as well as foods that are heavy, oily, and cold.

Balancing the Diet

The benefits of eating according to your constitution
- Better health, concentration, and memory
- Youthfulness
- More energy, endurance, and strength
- A gradual decrease in existing imbalances
- Prevention of imbalances
- Greater ability to handle stress and anxiety
- Saves money over time

- Improved sleep
- Better digestion, metabolism, and elimination
- Healthier skin, complexion
- Healthier progeny
- Stronger immune system
- Weight loss or gain (depending on what you need) and better sense of weight management
- Improved meditation and yoga practice
- More productive and happy life

Vata-Balancing Diet

Vata season is when weather is cold, windy, and dry. Depending on the location, vata season usually lasts from November through February. During this time of year, the qualities of vata naturally increase. Thus, one should take extra care during this time to take lots of warm food and drinks, as well as heavier and oilier foods. Eat more of the sweet, sour, and salty tastes. Avoid dry or cold food and drinks. Eat fewer of the pungent, bitter, and astringent tastes overall.

Favor foods that are: oily, heavy, warm, sweet, sour, and salty
- Beverages: almond milk, rice milk, grain beverages, aloe vera juice, apple cider, apricot, berry (not cranberry), carrot, cherry, grape, lemonade, mango, orange, papaya, peach, pineapple, sour juices, vegetable bouillon, miso broth
- • Herbal teas: ajwain, bancha, chamomile, clove, comfrey, elderflower, eucalyptus, fennel, fenugreek, ginger (fresh), hawthorn, juniper berry, lavender, lemon grass, licorice, marshmallow, oat straw, orange peel, pennyroyal, peppermint, rosehips, saffron, sage, sarsaparilla, sassafras, spearmint
- Condiments: chutney (mango), dulse, gomasio, hijiki, kelp, ketchup, lemon, lime, lime pickle, mango pickle, mayonnaise, mustard, pickles, scallions, seaweed, vinegar

- Dairy: raw butter, ghee, whole milk (cow and goat, avoid homogenized), lassi, cheese (cow and goat), fresh homemade paneer, cottage cheese, sour cream, yogurt
- Food supplements: aloe vera juice, bee pollen, amino acids, calcium, copper, iron, magnesium, royal jelly, spirulina, blue-green algae, vitamins A, B, B_{12}, C, D, E, and EFAs (essential fatty acids found in cold pressed oils from hemp seed, evening primrose, black currant seed, flax seed, borage)
- Fruits: apples (ripe and sweet, cooked), applesauce, avocado, banana, berries, cherries, coconut, dates, figs, grapefruit, grapes, kiwi, lemon, lime, mango, melon, oranges, papayas, peaches, pineapple, plums, pomegranate, prunes (soaked), raisins, rhubarb, strawberries, tamarind
- Grains: whole amaranth, cooked oats, spelt, quinoa, seitan (wheat meat), sprouted wheat bread (Essene style), white basmati rice,
- Legumes: mung beans, mung dal, tur dal, urad dal
- Nuts: almonds (soaked and peeled are best), black walnuts, brazil nuts, cashews, charole, coconut, filberts, hazelnuts, macadamia nuts, peanuts, pecans, pine nuts, pistachios, walnuts
- Oils: ghee, olive oil, sunflower oil, and other oils are generally okay; use coconut, sesame, and avocado oils externally only
- Seeds: chia and flax (soaked or sprouted), halva, hemp, pumpkin, sesame, sunflower
- Spices: ajwain, allspice, almond extract, anise, asafoetida (hing), basil, bay leaf, black pepper, cardamom, cayenne, cinnamon, clove, green coriander leaf, cumin, dill, fennel, fenugreek, garlic, ginger (especially fresh), marjoram, mint, mustard seeds, nutmeg, orange peel, oregano, paprika, parsley, peppermint, pippali, poppy seed, rosemary, saffron, savory, spearmint, star anise, tarragon, thyme, turmeric, vanilla, wintergreen
- Sweeteners: stevia, barley malt, fructose, fruit juice concentrates, honey, jaggery, molasses, rice syrup, raw sugar, sucanat, turbinado sugar

- Vegetables: asparagus, beets, red cabbage (cooked, in moderation), carrots, green chilies, cilantro, cucumber, daikon radish (cooked, in moderation), fennel (anise), garlic, green beans, dark leafy greens (cooked, in moderation), leeks, mustard greens, okra, olives (black), onions (cooked), parsnips, peas (cooked), sweet potato, pumpkin, radish (cooked), rutabaga, summer squash, taro root, watercress, zucchini

Reduce foods that are: dry, light, cold, spicy, bitter, astringent
Beans: reduce intake of beans, all of which increase vata, except mung dal

- Vegetables: raw vegetables, cruciferous vegetables, frozen, canned, fried foods, leftovers
- Spices: minimize use of chilies and red pepper
- Grains: reduce intake of barley, corn, millet, oats, rye
- Fruits: dry, light, or astringent fruits such as apples, berries, pears, and dried fruit
- Dairy: homogenized dairy, milk or yogurt with fruit or vegetables
- Avoid all iced/cold foods and drinks

Pitta-Balancing Diet

Pitta season is hot and dry, usually lasting from July through October. Again, this will vary depending on location. During this time, favor foods and drinks that are cooling. Eat foods of sweet, bitter, and astringent tastes. Include fresh, sweet fruits and vegetables that grow during the pitta season. Eat fewer pungent, sour, and salty foods. Avoid yogurt, cheese, tomatoes, vinegars, and hot spices, as they all greatly increase pitta.

Favor foods that are: oily, heavy, cold, bitter, sweet, and astringent

- Beverages: almond milk in moderation, rice milk, grain beverages, aloe vera juice, apple, apricot, berry, cherry, grape, mango, peach, pear, pomegranate, prune, mixed vegetable
- Herbal teas: alfalfa, bancha, barley, blackberry, borage, burdock, catnip, chamomile, chicory, comfrey, dandelion, fennel, ginger (fresh), hibiscus, hops, jasmine, kukicha, lavender, lemon balm, lemon grass, licorice, marshmallow, nettle, oat straw, passion flower, peppermint, raspberry, red clover, sarsaparilla, spearmint, strawberry, violet, wintergreen yarrow
- Condiments: chutney, coriander leaves, sprouts
- Dairy (raw is best): butter (unsalted), cow or goat cheese (soft, unsalted), ghee, whole cow and goat milk (avoid homogenized), lassi
- Food Supplements: aloe vera juice, blue-green algae, barley greens, brewer's yeast, calcium, magnesium, zinc, spirulina, vitamins D, E, and EFAs (essential fatty acids found in cold pressed oils from hemp seed, evening primrose, black currant seed, flax seed, borage), whey protein powder as a protein supplement (isolate only, do not use concentrates or hydrolyzed as the protein have been denatured)
- Fruits (ripe and sweet): apples, applesauce, apricots, avocado, berries (sweet), cherries, coconut, dates, figs, grapes (red and purple), mango, melons, oranges, papayas, pears, plums, pomegranate, prunes, raisins, watermelon
- Grains: whole amaranth and barley, cereals (dry), oat bran, oats, whole grain pasta, spelt, sprouted wheat bread (Essene style), tapioca, white basmati rice
- Legumes: adzuki beans, black beans, black-eyed peas, chickpeas (garbanzo beans), kidney beans, lentils (brown and red), lima beans, mung beans, mung dal, navy beans, peas (dried), pinto beans, split peas, white beans. *NOTE*: All legumes should be well-cooked
- Nuts: almonds (soaked and peeled), coconut

- Oils: coconut, ghee, olive oil
- Seeds: flax, hemp, pumpkin, sunflower
- Spices: basil (fresh), black pepper and fresh ginger (in moderation), cardamom, cinnamon, coriander, cumin, dill, fennel, mint, peppermint, spearmint, saffron, turmeric, rock salt
- Sweeteners: agave, barley malt, fruit juice, honey, maple syrup, rice syrup, stevia, raw sugar, sucanat, rock crystal sugar
- Vegetables: artichoke, asparagus, beets, bitter melon, broccoli, Brussels sprouts, cabbage, carrots, cauliflower, celery, cilantro, cucumber, dandelion greens, fennel, green beans, kale, dark leafy greens, leeks, okra, olives (black), onion (cooked), parsley, parsnip, peas, sweet potatoes, prickly pear leaves, pumpkin, rutabaga, spaghetti squash, sprouts, squash (winter and summer), taro root, wheat grass sprouts, zucchini

Reduce foods that are: dry, light, warm, salty, spicy, and sour
- Oils: reduce the use of almond, corn, and sesame oils
- Spices: avoid chili and cayenne
- Grains: reduce intake of brown rice, corn, millet, rye
- Fruits: reduce intake of sour fruits such as olives, unripe pineapples or persimmons, sour oranges, unripe bananas
- Sweeteners: avoid large quantities of honey.
- Dairy: reduce use of cheese, cultured buttermilk, sour cream, yogurt.

Kapha-Balancing Diet

Kapha season is the rainy and cool season that lasts from March through June, depending on location. During kapha season, eat foods that are light and oily. Take warm food and drinks. Eat foods that are pungent, bitter, and astringent in taste. Avoid foods that are sweet, salty, and sour flavored.

Favor foods that are: dry, warm, light, spicy, bitter, astringent

- Beverages: apple cider, apricot, berry, black tea (spiced), carrot, cherry, cranberry, grain beverages, grape, mango, peach, pear, pomegranate, prune
- Herbal teas: alfalfa, bancha, barley, blackberry, burdock, chamomile, chicory, clove, cinnamon, dandelion, fenugreek, ginger, hibiscus, jasmine, juniper berry, kukicha, lavender, lemon balm, lemon grass, nettle, passion flower, peppermint, raspberry, red clover, sassafras, spearmint, strawberry, wintergreen, yarrow, yerba mate
- Condiments: black pepper, chili peppers, chutney, coriander leaves, dulse, hijiki, horseradish, lemon, mustard (without vinegar), scallions, seaweed, sprouts
- Dairy (raw and organic): cottage cheese (from skimmed goat milk), lassi, non-fat goat milk, avoid homogenized dairy
- Food supplements: aloe vera juice, amino acids, barley green, bee pollen, blue-green algae, brewer's yeast, calcium, copper, iron, magnesium, zinc, royal jelly, spirulina, vitamins A, B, B$_{12}$, C, D, E, EFAs (essential fatty acids found in cold-pressed oils from hemp seed, evening primrose, black currant seed, flax seed, and borage oils), whey protein powder (isolate only—not concentrated or hydrolyzed)
- Fruits: apples, applesauce, apricots, berries, cherries, cranberries, dried fruit, grapes, guava, peaches, pears, persimmon, pomegranate, prunes, raisins
- Grains: (whole) barley, buckwheat, cereals (dry or puffed), corn (organic, non-GMO), couscous, granola, yellow and black millet, muesli, oat bran, polenta, quinoa, rye, basmati rice, spelt, sprouted wheat bread (Essene style), tapioca, wheat bran
- Legumes (well-cooked and with spices): adzuki beans, black beans, black-eyed peas, chick peas, lentils (red and brown), lima beans, mung beans, mung dal, navy beans, peas (dried), pinto beans, split peas, tur dal, white beans
- Oils: ghee, mustard oil, sesame oil

- Seeds: chia, flax, hemp, popcorn, pumpkin seeds, sunflower seeds
- Spices: all spices except salt, but especially fresh ginger
- Sweeteners: fruit juice, honey, stevia
- Vegetables: artichoke, asparagus, beet greens, beets in moderation, bitter melon, broccoli, brussel sprouts, cabbage, carrots in moderation, cauliflower, celery, cilantro, corn, daikon radish, dandelion greens, eggplant, fennel (anise), garlic, green beans, green chilies, horseradish, kale, kohlrabi, leafy greens (lettuces), leeks, mushrooms, mustard greens, okra, onions, parsley, peas, hot peppers, prickly pear, rutabaga, spinach, sprouts, summer squash, cooked tomatoes, turnip greens, turnips, watercress, wheat grass

Reduce foods that are: oily, cold, heavy, sweet, sour
- Nuts: avoid all nuts
- Oils: avoid large amounts of any oil
- Vegetables: cucumbers, okra, sweet potatoes, and tomatoes
- Spices: avoid salt and salty foods (pickles, chips)
- Grains: rice, wheat
- Fruits: bananas, coconuts, dates, figs, grapes, limes, mangoes, melons, oranges, and pineapples
- Sweeteners: avoid most sugar products
- Dairy: butter, cheese, cream, ice cream, sour cream, yogurt, and any excess of whole milk are not recommended

16

Self-Examination and Food Charts

These charts enable you to determine your individual constitution. To ensure accuracy, please be as honest as possible with yourself. Accurately determining your constitution will assist you in following a proper lifestyle regime. Balancing your doshas is essential to living a happy and healthy life. Remember that no one is purely one type.

Please do not make definitive conclusions about yourself based on these charts. They are generalizations meant for educational purposes and as a guide for self-examination. On each line, choose the aspect that applies most to you. For more specific diagnosis, please see an experienced Ayurvedic practitioner who can properly assess your constitutional presentation.

Prakriti – Your Individual Constitution

Aspects	Vata	Pitta	Kapha
Activity	very active	moderate	slow
Appetite	low, variable	strong	steady
Body frame	thin	medium	large
Body weight	light	moderate	heavy
Concentration	short-term only, poor	above average, good	long-term, excellent
Disease pattern	nervous, anxiety, pain	heat-related	mucous-related

Dreams	fearful, active	angry, fiery	watery, calm
Elimination	dry, hard, con-stipated	oily, loose, soft	oily, thick, slow
Emotions	fearful, insecure	angry, irritable	attached, greedy
Endurance	fair	good	high
Eyes	small, dry, active	sharp, penetrat-ing	big, attractive
Hair color	brown, black	red/grey	dark
Hair quantity	average	thin	thick
Hair type	dry	medium thick-ness	oily
Memory	good short-term	good	good long-term
Mental	quick, restless	sharp, aggres-sive	calm, steady, stable
Pulse pattern	swan, feeble, thready	frog, moderate, jumping	swan, broad, slow
Skin	dry, rough	soft, oily	thick, oily
Sleep	light, disturbed	sound, medium	deep, long
Strength	fair	above average	excellent
Talking	rapid, scattered	clear, fast, sharp	slow, clear, sweet
Teeth	protruding, crooked	medium-sized, soft	large, strong
Thirst	variable	excessive	slight
Thoughts	erratic	consistent	steady pace, focused
Voice	high-pitched, feeble	medium-pitched	low-pitched
Totals:			

Subdosha Charts

Place a check mark next to the description that applies to you.

Vata	
Prana Vata	
anxiety	
asthma	
dehydration	
emaciation	
hiccups	
hoarseness	
insomnia	
loss of voice	
senility	
shortness of breath	
tension headaches	
tuberculosis	
wasting	
worry	
Total Prana Vata	
Udana Vata	
cancer	
dry cough	
dry eyes	
earaches	
fatigue	

lack of enthusiasm	
overexcitement	
sore throat	
speech defects	
stuttering	
tonsillitis	
weakness	
Total Udana Vata	
Samana Vata	
dehydration	
diarrhea	
indigestion	
low energy	
poor nutrition	
rapid digestion	
slow digestion	
Total Samana Vata	
Apana Vata	
birth trauma, difficult birth	
constipation	
diabetes	
diarrhea	
dysmenorrhea	
low back pain	
menstrual disorders	

sexual dysfunction			hostility	
stillbirth			jaundice	
Total Apana Vata			liver disease	
			low blood pressure	
Vyana Vata			rashes	
arthritis			Total Ranjaka Pitta	
frequent blinking				
heart irregularities			**Sadhaka Pitta**	
joint cracking			Emotional disturbance	
joint pain			Heart attack	
nervousness			Indecision	
poor circulation			Low intelligence	
Total Vyana Vata			Poor memory	
			Total Sadhaka Pitta	
Pitta				
Pachaka Pitta			**Alochaka Pitta**	
acidity			Eye diseases	
addictions			Red/irritated eyes	
cravings			Anger	
heartburn			Vision problems	
indigestion			**Total Alochaka Pitta**	
ulcers				
Total Pachaka Pitta			**Bhrajaka Pitta**	
			Acne	
Ranjaka Pitta			All skin disorders	
anemia			Boils/Abscesses	
anger			Hot skin	
blood disorders			Inflammation	

Poor memory				
Rashes		**Tarpaka Kapha**	
Skin cancer		Depression	
Total Bhrajaka Pitta		Headaches	
		Impairment of senses	
Kapha		Irritability	
Kledaka Kapha		Loss of smell	
Bloating		Sinus problems	
Excess mucous in stomach		**Total Tarpaka Kapha**	
Slow digestion			
Total Kledaka Kapha		**Sleshaka Kapha**	
		Chest congestion	
Avalambaka Kapha		Lethargy	
Asthma		Loose joints	
Back pain		Stiffness of joints and body	
Chest/lung congestion		Swelling	
Heart pain		**Total Sleshaka Kapha**	
Lethargy			
Stiffness			
Total Avalambaka Kapha			
Bodhaka Kapha			
Diabetes			
Food sensitivity			
General congestion			
Loss of taste			
Obesity			
Total Bodhaka Kapha			

Three Gunas Constitutional Chart

Place a checkmark next to the one that most accurately applies to you. Again, be honest with yourself. If the result is not how you wish it to be, you can use this as a tool for self-improvement, growth and inner expansion.

Aspects	Satva	Rajas	Tamas
Alcohol	never	occasionally	often
Anger	rarely	occasionally	often
Attachment	little	moderate	high
Cleanliness	high	moderate	low
Concentration	strong	moderate	lacking, poor
Contentment	usually	occasionally	never
Creativity	high	moderate	poor
Daily exercise	always	occasionally	rarely
Depression	rarely/never	occasionally	often
Desire/lust	little	moderate	excessive
Detachment	high	moderate	low/none
Diet	pure vegetarian/ vegan	some meat	diet high in meat
Discrimination	high	moderate	low/none
Drugs	never	occasionally	often
Fear	rarely	occasionally	often
Forgiveness	easily	forgives with time	holds grudges
Greed	little	moderate	high
Love	unconditional	personal	selfish, lacking
Mantra/prayer	daily	occasionally	never
Meditation	daily	occasionally	never
Memory	strong	moderate	poor
Non-coveting	always	moderate/ occasionally	rarely

Non-stealing	always	occasionally	rarely
Non-violence	always	occasionally	rarely
Peace of mind	almost always	moderate/ occasionally	rarely
Pride/ego	modest/humble	fluctuating	vanity
Self-discipline	high	moderate	low/none
Self-study/ reflection	high	moderate	low/none
Sense control	good	moderate	weak
Sensory input	calm, pure	mixed	disturbed
Seva (selfless service)	regularly	moderate/ occasionally	poor/rarely
Speech	peaceful, serene	excited, agi-tated	lifeless, dull
Spiritual study	daily	occasionally	never
Truthfulness	always	usually	rarely
Will power	strong	fluctuates	weak
Work ethic	selfless	personal gain	lazy
Totals			

Food Charts

* means eat in moderation
** means eat rarely

Vata			
FRUITS – Advisable *Most sweet fruit*	FRUITS – Avoid *Most dried fruit*	VEGETABLES – Advisable *In general, vegetables should be cooked.*	VEGETABLES – Avoid *Frozen, raw or dried vegetables*
• apples (cooked) • applesauce • apricots • avocado • bananas • berries • cherries • coconut • dates (fresh) • figs (fresh) • grapefruit • grapes • kiwi • lemons • limes • mangoes • melons • oranges • papayas • peaches • pineapple • plums • prunes (soaked)	• apples (raw) • cranberries • dates (dry) • figs (dry) • pears • pomegranates • prunes (dry) • raisins (dry) • watermelon	• asparagus • beets • cabbage (cooked) • carrots • cauliflower* • cilantro • cucumber • daikon radish* • fennel (anise) • garlic • green beans • green chilies • Jerusalem artichoke* • leafy greens * • leeks • lettuce* • mustard greens* • okra • olives, black • onions (cooked)*	• artichoke • beet greens** • bitter melon • broccoli • Brussels sprouts • burdock root • cabbage (raw) • cauliflower (raw) • celery • corn (fresh)** • dandelion greens • eggplant • horseradish** • kale • kohlrabi • olives, green • onions (raw) • peppers, sweet and hot

Vata			
FRUITS – Advisable *Most sweet fruit*	**FRUITS –** Avoid *Most dried fruit*	**VEGETABLES –** **Advisable** *In general, vegetables should be cooked.*	**VEGETABLES –** **Avoid** *Frozen, raw or dried vegetables*
• raisins (soaked) • rhubarb • strawberries • tamarind		• parsley* • parsnip • peas (cooked) • potatoes, sweet• pumpkin • radishes (cooked)* • rutabaga • spaghetti squash* • spinach*	• potatoes, white • prickly pear (fruit and leaves) • radish (raw) • sprouts • tomatoes (cooked)** • turnips • wheat grass

Vata			
LEGUMES – Advisable	**LEGUMES –** Avoid	**DAIRY –** **Advisable** *Most dairy is good.*	**DAIRY –** **Avoid**
• lentils (red)* • mung beans • mung dal • soy cheese* • soy milk* • soy sauce* • soy sausages* • tofu* • tur dal • urad dal	• adzuki beans • black beans • black-eyed peas • chick peas (garbanzo beans) • kidney beans • lentils, (brown) • lima beans	• butter • buttermilk • cheese (hard)* • cheese (soft) • cottage cheese • cow's milk • ghee • goat's cheese • goat's milk	• cow's milk (powdered) • goat's milk (powdered) • yogurt (plain, frozen or with fruit)

Vata			
LEGUMES – Advisable	LEGUMES – Avoid	DAIRY – Advisable *Most dairy is good.*	DAIRY – Avoid
	• miso** • navy beans • peas (dried) • pinto beans • soybeans • soy flour • soy powder • split peas • tempeh • white beans	• ice cream* • sour cream* • yogurt (diluted and spiced)*	

Vata			
NUTS – Advisable *In moderation*	NUTS – Avoid	SEEDS – Advisable	SEEDS – Avoid
• almonds • black walnuts • brazil nuts • cashews • charole • coconut • filberts • hazelnuts • macadamia nuts • peanuts • pecans • pine nuts • pistachios • walnuts	• none	• chia • flax • halva • hemp • pumpkin • sesame • sunflower • tahini	• popcorn • psyllium**

Vata			
GRAINS – Advisable	GRAINS – Avoid	BEVERAGES – Advisable	BEVERAGES – Avoid
• amaranth* • durham flour • oats (cooked) • pancakes • quinoa • rice (all kinds) • seitan (wheat meat) • sprouted wheat bread (Essene) • wheat	• barley • bread (made with yeast) • buckwheat • cereals (cold, dry or puffed) • corn • couscous • crackers • granola • millet • muesli • oat bran • oats (dry) • pasta** • polenta** • rice cakes** • rye • sago • spelt • tapioca • wheat bran	• alcohol (beer or wine)* • almond milk • aloe vera juice • apple cider • apricot juice • berry juice (except for cranberry) • carob* • carrot juice • cherry juice • grain beverage (coffee substitute) • grape juice • grapefruit juice • hot spiced milk • lemonade • mango juice • miso broth • orange juice • papaya juice • peach nectar • pineapple juice • rice milk • sour juices • soy milk (hot and well-spiced)*	• apple juice • black tea • caffeinated beverages • carbonated drinks • chocolate milk • coffee • cold dairy drinks • cranberry juice • iced tea • icy cold drinks • herbal teas: alfalfa** barley** basil** blackberry borage** burdock cinnamon** corn silk dandelion ginseng hibiscus hops** jasmine** lemon balm** • mixed vegetable juice

Vata			
GRAINS – Advisable	**GRAINS – Avoid**	**BEVERAGES – Advisable**	**BEVERAGES – Avoid**
		• herbal teas: ajwan bancha catnip* chamomile chicory chrysanthe-mum* clove	• pear juice • pomegranate juice • prune juice** • soy milk (cold) • tomato juice** • vegetable bouillon

Vata			
OILS – Advisable *Most suitable at top*	**OILS – Avoid**	**SPICES – Advisable** *Almost all spices are good.*	**SPICES – Avoid**
• sesame • ghee • olive • most other oils *External use only:* • coconut • avocado	• flax seed	• ajwan • allspice • almond extract • anise • asafoetida (hing) • basil • bay leaf • black pepper • cardamom • cayenne* • cinnamon • cloves • coriander • cumin • curry leaves • dill	• caraway

Vata			
OILS – **Advisable** *Most suitable at top*	OILS – **Avoid**	SPICES – **Advisable** *Almost all spices are good.*	SPICES – **Avoid**
		• fennel • fenugreek* • garlic • ginger • mace • marjoram • mint • mustard seeds • nutmeg • orange peel • oregano • paprika • parsley • peppermint • pippali • poppy seeds • rosemary • saffron • savory • spearmint • star anise • tarragon • thyme • turmeric • vanilla • wintergreen	

Vata			
CONDI-MENTS – Advisable	CONDI-MENTS – Avoid	SWEETEN-ERS – Advisable	SWEETEN-ERS – Avoid
• chutney, mango (sweet or spicy) • cilantro* • dulse • gomasio • hijiki • kelp • ketchup • kombu • lemon • lime • mayonnaise • mustard • pickles (lime pickle, mango pickle) • salt • scallions • seaweed • soy sauce • sprouts* • tamari	• chocolate • horseradish	• barley malt • fructose • fruit juice concentrate • honey (raw and unpro-cessed) • jaggery • molasses • rice syrup • sucanat • turbinado	• maple syrup** • white sugar

Vata	
FOOD SUPPLEMENTS – Advisable	FOOD SUPPLEMENTS – Avoid
• aloe vera juice* • amino acids • bee pollen • minerals: calcium, copper, iron, magnesium, zinc • royal jelly • spirulina • blue-green algae • vitamins A, B, B$_{12}$, C, D and E	• barley green • brewer's yeast

Pitta			
FRUITS – Advisable *Most sweet fruit*	FRUITS – Avoid *Most sour fruit*	VEGETABLES – Advisable *Most sweet and bitter vegetables*	VEGETABLES – Avoid *Most pungent vegetables*
• apples (sweet) • applesauce • apricots (sweet) • avocado • berries (sweet) • cherries (sweet) • coconut • dates • figs • grapes (red and purple) • limes*	• apples (sour) • apricots (sour) • bananas • berries (sour) • cherries (sour) • cranberries • grapefruit • grapes (green) • kiwi** • lemons • mangoes (green) • oranges (sour)	• artichoke • asparagus • beets (cooked) • bitter melon • broccoli • Brussels sprouts • cabbage • carrots (cooked) • carrots (raw)* • cauliflower • celery • cilantro • cucumber	• beet greens • beets, raw • burdock root • corn (fresh)** • daikon radish • eggplant** • garlic • green chilies • horseradish • kohlrabi** • leeks (raw) • mustard greens • olives (green) • onions (raw)

Pitta			
FRUITS – Advisable *Most sweet fruit*	FRUITS – Avoid *Most sour fruit*	VEGETABLES – Advisable *Most sweet and bitter vegetables*	VEGETABLES – Avoid *Most pungent vegetables*
• mangoes (ripe) • melons • oranges (sweet) • papayas* • pears • pineapple (sweet) • pomegranates • prunes • raisins • watermelon	• peaches • persimmons • pineapple (sour) • plums (sour) • prickly pear • rhubarb • strawberries • tamarind	• dandelion greens • fennel (anise) • green beans • Jerusalem artichokes • kale • leafy greens • leeks (cooked) • lettuce • okra • olives (black) • onions (cooked) • parsley • parsnips • peas • peppers (sweet) • potatoes (sweet, white)	• peppers (hot) • radishes (raw) • spinach (cooked)** • spinach (raw) • tomatoes • turnip greens • turnips

Pitta			
LEGUMES – Advisable	LEGUMES – Avoid	DAIRY – Advisable	DAIRY – Avoid
• adzuki beans • black beans • black-eyed peas • chick peas (garbanzo beans) • kidney beans • lentils (brown, red) • lima beans • mung beans • mung dal • navy beans • peas (dried) • pinto beans • soy beans • soy cheese • soy flour* • soy milk • soy powder* • split peas • tempeh • tofu • white beans	• miso • soy sauce • soy sausages • tur dal • urad dal	• butter (unsalted) • cheese (soft, not aged, unsalted) • cottage cheese • cow's milk • ghee • goat's cheese (soft and unsalted) • goat's milk • ice cream • yogurt (freshly made and diluted)*	• butter (salted) • buttermilk • cheese (hard) • sour cream • yogurt (plain, frozen or with fruit)

Pitta			
GRAINS – Advisable	**GRAINS –** Avoid	**BEVERAGES –** Advisable	**BEVERAGES –** Avoid
• amaranth • barley • cereal, dry • couscous • crackers • durham flour • granola • oat bran • oats (cooked) • pancakes • pasta • rice (basmati, white, wild) • rice cakes • sago • seitan (wheat meat) • spelt • sprouted wheat bread (Essene) • tapioca • wheat • wheat bran	• bread (with yeast) • buckwheat • corn • millet • muesli** • oats (dry) • polenta** • quinoa • rice (brown)** • rye	• almond milk • aloe vera juice • apple juice • apricot juice • berry juice (sweet) • carob • cherry juice (sweet) • cool dairy drinks • grain beverage (coffee substitute) • grape juice • hot, spiced milk* • mango juice • miso broth* • mixed vegetable juice • orange juice* • peach nectar • pear juice • pomegranate juice • prune juice • rice milk • soy milk • vegetable bouillon • herbal teas: alfalfa bancha	• apple cider • berry juice (sour) • caffeinated beverages • carbonated drinks • carrot juice • cherry juice (sour) • chocolate milk • coffee • cranberry juice • grapefruit juice • iced tea • iced drinks • lemonade • papaya juice • tomato juice • sour juices • herbal teas: ajwan basil** cinnamon* clove eucalyptus fenugreek ginger (dry) ginseng hawthorne hyssop

Pitta			
GRAINS – Advisable	GRAINS – Avoid	BEVERAGES – Advisable	BEVERAGES – Avoid
		barley blackberry borage burdock catnip chamomile	juniper berry pennyroyal

Pitta			
NUTS – Advisable	NUTS – Avoid	SEEDS – Advisable	SEEDS – Avoid
• almonds (soaked and peeled) • charole • coconut	• almonds (with skin) • black walnuts • brazil nuts • cashews • filberts • hazelnuts • macadamia nuts • peanuts • pecans • pine nuts • pistachios • walnuts	• flax • halva • hemp • popcorn (no salt, buttered) • psyllium • pumpkin* • sunflower	• chia • sesame • tahini

Pitta			
OILS – Advisable *Most suitable at top*	OILS – Avoid	SPICES – Advisable	SPICES – Avoid
• sunflower • ghee • canola • olive • soy • flax seed • primrose • walnut *External use only:* • avocado • coconut	• almond • apricot • corn • safflower • sesame	• basil (fresh) • black pepper* • caraway* • cardamom* • cinnamon • coriander • cumin • curry leaves • dill • fennel • ginger (fresh) • mint • neem leaves* • orange peel* • parsley* • peppermint • saffron • spearmint • tarragon* • turmeric • vanilla* • wintergreen	• ajwan • allspice • almond extract • anise • asafoetida (hing) • basil (dry) • bay leaf • cayenne • cloves • fenugreek • garlic • ginger (dry) • mace • marjoram • mustard seeds • nutmeg • oregano • paprika • pippali • poppy seeds • rosemary • sage • savory • star anise • thyme

Pitta			
CONDI-MENTS – Advisable	CONDI-MENTS – Avoid	SWEETEN-ERS – Advisable	SWEETEN-ERS – Avoid
• black pepper* • chutney, mango (sweet) • cilantro* • dulse* • hijiki • kombu* • lime* • sprouts • tamari*	• chili pepper • chocolate • chutney, mango (spicy) • gomasio • horseradish • kelp • ketchup • lemon • lime pickle • mango pickle • mayonnaise • mustard • pickles • salt** • scallions • seaweed • soy sauce • vinegar	• barley malt • fructose • fruit juice concentrate • maple syrup • rice syrup • sucanat • turbinado	• honey** (raw, unprocessed) • jaggery • molasses • white sugar**

Pitta	
FOOD SUPPLEMENTS – Advisable	FOOD SUPPLEMENTS – Avoid
• aloe vera juice • barley green • brewer's yeast • minerals: calcium, magnesium, zinc • spirulina • blue-green algae • vitamins D and E	• amino acids • bee pollen** • royal jelly** • minerals: copper, iron, vitamins A, B, B_{12}, and C

Kapha			
FRUITS – **Advisable** *Most astringent fruit*	**FRUITS –** **Avoid** *Most sweet and sour fruit*	**VEGETABLES** **–** **Advisable** *Most bitter and pungent veg-etables*	**VEGETABLES** **–** **Avoid** *Most sweet and juicy vegetables*
• apples • applesauce • apricots • berries • cherries • cranberries • figs (dry)* • grapes* • lemons* • limes* • peaches • pears • persimmons • pomegranates • prunes • raisins • strawberries*	• avocado • bananas • coconut • dates • figs (fresh) • grapefruit • kiwi • mangoes** • melons • oranges • papayas • pineapple • plums • rhubarb • tamarind • watermelon	• artichoke • asparagus • beet greens • beets • bitter melon • broccoli • Brussels sprouts • burdock root • cabbage • carrots • cauliflower • celery • cilantro • corn • daikon radish • dandelion greens • eggplant • fennel (anise) • garlic • green beans • green chilies • horseradish • Jerusalem artichoke • kale • kohlrabi • leafy greens • leeks • lettuce	• cucumber • olives • parsnips** • potatoes (sweet) • squash (win-ter) • taro root • tomatoes (raw) • zucchini

Kapha			
FRUITS – **Advisable** *Most astringent fruit*	**FRUITS –** **Avoid** *Most sweet and sour fruit*	**VEGETABLES –** **Advisable** *Most bitter and pungent veg-etables*	**VEGETABLES –** **Avoid** *Most sweet and juicy vegetables*
		• mustard greens • okra • onions • pumpkin	

Kapha			
LEGUMES – **Advisable**	**LEGUMES –** **Avoid**	**DAIRY –** **Advisable**	**DAIRY –** **Avoid**
• adzuki beans • black beans • black-eyed peas • chick peas (garbanzo beans) • lentils (red and brown) • lima beans • mung beans* • mung dal* • navy beans • peas (dried) • pinto beans • soy milk • soy sausages • split peas • tempeh • tofu (cooked)* • tur dal • white beans	• kidney beans • miso • soy beans • soy cheese • soy flour • soy powder • soy sauce • tofu (raw) • urad dal	• buttermilk* • cottage cheese (from skimmed goat's milk) • ghee* • goat's cheese (unsalted and not aged)* • goat's milk (skim) • yogurt (dilut-ed)	• butter (salted) • butter (unsalted)** • cheese (soft and hard) • cow's milk • ice cream • sour cream • yogurt (plain, frozen or with fruit)

Kapha			
NUTS – Advisable *In moderation*	NUTS – Avoid	SEEDS – Advisable	SEEDS – Avoid
• almonds • black walnuts • brazil nuts • cashews • charole • coconut • filberts • hazelnuts • macadamia nuts • peanuts • pecans • pine nuts • pistachios • walnuts	• none	• chia • flax • halva • hemp • pumpkin • sesame • sunflower • tahini	• popcorn • psyllium**

Kapha			
GRAINS – Advisable	GRAINS – Avoid	BEVERAGES – Advisable	BEVERAGES – Avoid
• amaranth* • barley • buckwheat • cereal (cold, dry or puffed) • corn • couscous • crackers • durham flour* • granola • millet • muesli	• bread (made with yeast) • oats (cooked) • pancakes • pasta** • rice (brown, white) • rice cakes** • wheat	• aloe vera juice • apple cider • apple juice* • apricot juice • berry juice • black tea (spiced) • carob • carrot juice • cherry juice (sweet) • cranberry juice	• almond milk • caffeinated beverages** • carbonated drinks • cherry juice (sour) • coffee • dairy drinks (cold) • grapefruit juice

Kapha			
GRAINS – Advisable	**GRAINS – Avoid**	**BEVERAGES – Advisable**	**BEVERAGES – Avoid**

• oat bran
• oats (dry)
• polenta
• quinoa*
• rice (basmati, wild)*
• rye
• sango
• seitan (wheat meat)
• spelt*
• sprouted wheat bread (Essene)
• tapioca
• wheat bran
		• hot spiced milk*
		• grain beverage (substitute coffee)
		• grape juice
		• herbal teas:
		  alfalfa
		  bancha
		  barley
		  blackberry
		  burdock
		  chamomile
		  chicory
		  cinnamon
		  clove
		• mango juice
		• peach nectar
		• pear juice
		• pineapple juice*
		• pomegranate juice
		• prune juice
		• soy milk (hot and well-spiced)
			• herbal teas:
			  marshmallow
			  rosehip**
			• iced tea
			• icy cold drinks
			• lemonade
			• miso broth
			• orange juice
			• papaya juice
			• rice milk
			• sour juices
			• soy milk (cold)
			• tomato juice

Kapha			
OILS – Advisable *Most suitable* *at top*	OILS – Avoid	SPICES – Advisable *All spices are* *good.*	SPICES – Avoid

• corn
• canola
• sunflower
• ghee
• almond
	• apricot
	• avocado
	• coconut
	• flax seed**
	• olive
	• primrose
	• safflower
	• sesame
	• soy
	• walnut
		• ajwan
		• allspice
		• almond
		  extract
		• anise
		• asafoetida
		  (hing)
		• basil
		• bay leaf
		• black pepper
		• caraway
		• cardamom
		• cayenne
		• cinnamon
		• cloves
		• coriander
		• cumin
		• curry leaves
		• dill
		• fennel*
		• fenugreek
		• garlic
		• ginger
		• mace
		• marjoram
		• mint
		• mustard seeds
		• neem leaves
		• nutmeg
		• orange peel
		• oregano
		• paprika	

Kapha			
OILS – Advisable *Most suitable at top*	OILS – Avoid	SPICES – Advisable *All spices are good.*	SPICES – Avoid
		• parsley • peppermint • pippali • poppy seeds • rosemary • saffron • sage • savory • spearmint • tarragon • thyme • turmeric • vanilla*	

Kapha			
CONDI-MENTS – Advisable	CONDI-MENTS – Avoid	SWEETEN-ERS – Advisable	SWEETEN-ERS – Avoid
• black pepper • chili peppers • chutney, mango (spicy) • cilantro • dulse* • hijiki* • horseradish • lemon* • mustard (without vinegar) • scallions • seaweed* • sprouts*	• chocolate • chutney, mango (sweet) • gomasio • kelp • ketchup** • lime • mayonnaise • pickles • salt • soy sauce • tamari • vinegar	• fruit juice concentrate • honey (raw, unprocessed)	• barley malt • fructose • jaggery • maple syrup • molasses • rice syrup • sucanat • turbinado sugar • white sugar

Kapha	
FOOD SUPPLEMENTS – Advisable	FOOD SUPPLEMENTS – Avoid
• aloe vera juice • amino acids • barley green • bee pollen • brewer's yeast • minerals: calcium, copper, iron, magnesium, zinc • royal jelly • spirulina • blue-green algae • vitamins A, B, B_{12}, C, D and E	• minerals: potassium

17

The Real Goal of Life

Our body is perishable. Only the soul is permanent. This is a rented body. We will be asked to leave at any time. Before that, we should look for a place in a permanent abode. Then, when we leave the body, we will move to that permanent abode, the eternal house of God. No one brings anything into this world, nor does anyone take anything with him when he leaves.

- Amma

Knowing that we are in "rented" bodies, we sense that there must be some higher purpose or goal for us than to simply enjoy the material comforts and pleasures of a temporary existence. Ayurveda and yoga state that there are four goals or desires in life that are considered legitimate or worthwhile. These are referred to as the *purusharthas*, and are considered applicable to every human being. These universal, basic desires are at the heart of all other desires.

The four goals or desires identified in the *shastras* (Vedic scriptures) are *kama, artha, dharma, and moksha.* All beings pursue one or all of these goals. Once a goal has been identified, we must contemplate the right means and then work to attain it. The goal should be clear, cherished, and sought with intensity and awareness. The degree to which we are seeking any of these four goals determines the balance and harmony we keep in life as well as the success we will achieve. The first three are catalysts for the fourth and ultimate goal of moksha (Self-realization). In order to attain any of these goals, we need to be strong, healthy, and filled with vitality and love. We need a healthy body as well as a healthy heart and clear mind.

Cleansing and fasting are the strongest appeal to the human being's natural powers of healing, on both a physical and spiritual level.

The Four Goals of Life

1. **Kama** (desire): Kama means satisfying legitimate desires with the assistance of one's possessions (artha).
2. **Artha** (wealth): Artha means the accumulation of wealth or possessions while fulfilling one's duties (dharma).
3. **Dharma** (career/life path): In addition to one's career or work, dharma means the fulfillment of one's duties to society. Ideally, one's career and societal duties are in alignment with one another.
4. **Moksha** (liberation): Moksha is Self-realization, and the realization that there is more to life than duties, possessions, and desires (dharma, artha, kama).

Kama

Translated literally as "desire," kama is the achievement of one's personal aspirations. All ambitions and desires, including lust, are considered kama; however, on a deeper level, kama represents the innate urge to attain one's aspiration.

For most creatures, enjoyment is the essence of their existence. Everyone wants to be happy and free from suffering. However, in the world today, most people seek happiness from external things. Real, lasting, un-fluctuating happiness comes only from deep within one's Self, and not from external objects. External objects do serve valid purposes, but one should understand their proper place in life.

For example, many people in the world today crave sexual satisfaction; this desire guides many of their decisions and actions. Eventually, one must realize that the body and the world will inevitably perish. The true source of happiness lies within. This doesn't mean we shouldn't enjoy the objects of the world; it simply means that we need to understand their transient nature and let go of our attachment to those things. It is the attachment to external objects that is the cause of our suffering. Amma wants us to remember: "Nothing in this material world is everlasting. Everything can go at any time. Therefore, live in this world with the alertness of a bird perched on a dry twig. The bird knows that the twig can break at any time."

Artha

Artha means wealth or prosperity. It refers to the accumulation of wealth. We need a certain amount of wealth to live our lives. Our basic necessities include clothing, food, shelter, and medicine when we are sick. Money represents a means of attaining resources. It facilitates the fulfillment of our desires and duties, and helps bring about a sense of security. Wealth essentially allows us to function comfortably in life.

One's attitude toward money and work should be properly considered. If we are selfless and share what blessings we have with others, then there will always be enough for the whole world. If we hoard wealth, then people will go without and suffer. The universe is compassionate. Mother Earth is compassionate. She will always provide for her children if her bounty is not abused.

The sage Sri Adi Shankaracharya wrote in the *Vivekachudamani* (The Crest Jewel of Discrimination), "There is no hope of immortality by means of riches – such indeed is the declaration of the Vedas. Hence it is clear that works cannot be the cause of liberation."

If we are fortunate enough to have accumulated some wealth and we regularly donate a portion of our earnings to charitable causes that alleviate suffering, then we are performing a form of selfless service (Karma Yoga). Amma says, "There is a difference between buying medicine to relieve your own pain and going out to get medicine for someone else. The latter shows a loving heart." The poverty of countries such as India is astounding. People suffer because they can't even afford a ten-rupee painkiller to alleviate a headache. Some people even die because they can't afford a three-dollar antibiotic. If we use a portion of our income to help such people, our lives will become blessed. When we serve selflessly, we start to feel the presence of the Divine blossoming within our hearts.

Dharma

Dharayati iti dharma means "that which sustains all." Dharma refers to right conduct and a righteous way of living in the world. Dharma can simply refer to our career or vocation, but it can also refer to how we live in the world. Following the path of right conduct and living a life of harmony and love is the real dharma. In its highest sense, dharma means the ultimate way or the natural law or way of things. Just as it is the dharma of the sun to shine and the dharma of the planets to revolve around the sun, humans have a dharma to follow. When followed carefully and with awareness, dharma will carry us across the ocean of samsara. To follow one's dharma is to surrender to the cosmic flow and natural law of the universe. The true role of spirituality is to reveal to each individual his or her unique dharma. However, at present, the involvement of the ego often relegates dharma to dogma and ritual. Dharma is much more than religion. It transcends all castes, limited viewpoints, and philosophies. It is a way of life that enables peaceful co-existence with others and is conducive to the attainment of all our worldly and spiritual goals. The way each of us manifests dharma is unique. Mark Twain wrote, "Always do right. This will gratify some and astonish the rest." Everyone has unique talents for a specific reason. Amma says, "You cannot simply adopt any path that you feel like. Each one will have a path, which they followed in the previous birth. Only if that path is followed will one progress in one's practice."

If we put forth self-effort, God's grace will soon follow. Part of this effort involves looking within and finding our own path, our dharma. It is our responsibility to ourselves, to the world, and to all of creation to allow our talents to be manifested in the world. The world is God's beautiful creation, and each person has a role to play in it. Playing our role in the world's perfection is the pinnacle of dharma, and in order to do so, we must not act blindly or apathetically. When each of us follows our individual and universal dharma, truth and righteousness will be restored to the world.

Nature is a huge flower garden. The animals, birds, trees, plants, and people are the garden's fully blossomed flowers of diverse colors. The beauty of this garden is complete only when all of these exist as a unity, thereby spreading the vibrations of love and oneness. Let us work together to prevent these diverse flowers from withering away so that the garden may remain eternally beautiful.

~ Amma

Eco-Dharma

Forget not that the earth delights to feel your bare feet and the winds long to play with your hair.

~ Kahlil Gibran

To find the universal elements enough; to find the air and the water exhilarating; to be refreshed by a morning walk or an evening saunter; to be thrilled by the stars at night; to be elated over a bird's nest or a wildflower in spring – these are some of the rewards of the simple life.

~ John Burroughs, Naturalist (1837-1921)

Thousands of years ago, humans lived in perfect harmony with nature. Over time, this harmony was lost. It is impossible to disrespect Mother Nature and simultaneously embody true health and consciousness. The goals of Ayurveda and yoga cannot be realized without love and respect for Mother Earth.

The modern age has seen such a major decline of dharma that the environment is in dire need of help. The planet and humanity are at a fragile breaking point where anything could happen. Resources are quickly diminishing while war and sickness are constantly on the rise. The population is increasing at an alarming rate. The gap between the "haves" and the "have-nots" is continuously widening. There is a growing destruction of forests, wilderness, rivers, lakes, clean air, and nutritious food. Pollution, desertification, and extinction of plants and animals are rapidly on the rise. The cause of this chaos and destruction is the human ego. Due to ignorance, greed, and pride, the fragile balance of life on planet Earth is being threatened. All of the other species of life on the planet live in balance with nature. It is the humans who are responsible for the chaos and destruction. If we continue to abuse Mother Earth, She will soon become uninhabitable for humans.

Fortunately, it is not too late. There is still hope. If we come together now as a one-world family, united in love, we can restore the lost harmony. We can heal the wounds inflicted on each other and our Mother Earth. The rivers can again flow clean and freely. We can all eat healthful, nutritious, life-giving foods. It is possible for all beings to live together in peace and happiness with the Earth. Just as the health of a mother greatly affects the health of her nursing baby, the health and happiness of Mother Earth directly affects the health and happiness of Her children—us. It is our dharma to heal our Mother Earth, thus healing ourselves. It is our dharma to heal ourselves, thus healing our Mother Earth.

As Walt Whitman said, "Now I see the secret of the making of the best persons. It is to grow in the open air and to eat and sleep with the Earth." In truth, humans have only one dharma to follow: seeking liberation or union with God, or the Self. All other dharma leads to this one. However, without a habitable planet, this goal is not possible. We can put our priorities in order by asking ourselves what Henry David Thoreau once asked: "What is the use of a house if you haven't got a planet to put it on?" Mother Earth is our home and She is in a state of emergency. She has been screaming and many people are not listening. It is our responsibility to preserve the Earth.

As Chief Seattle said, "The Earth does not belong to us, we belong to the Earth." Mother Earth is gravely ill. We have an obligation to both our ancestors and our children: to protect what our ancestors cultivated, and to preserve what our children's children will inherit. Global unification is necessary, coming together to restore the lost harmony. By following the principles of eco-dharma, we gain more awareness of how we impact the environment by the products we buy and use. The ancient Cree prophecy says, "Only after the last tree has been cut down, only after the last river has been poisoned, only after the last fish has been caught, only then will one find that money cannot be eaten." We often make money our first priority while neglecting the environment; it is time to re-evaluate our motivations and actions.

> *"Life becomes fulfilled when humankind and nature*
> *move together, hand and hand in harmony. When*
> *melody and rhythm complement each other, the*
> *music becomes beautiful and pleasing to the ear.*
> *Likewise, when people live in accordance with the*
> *laws of nature, life becomes like a beautiful song"*
>
> ~ *Amma*

Moksha

Moksha means "freedom from the bonds of ignorance." The jiva (individual soul) can merge with atman (Supreme/Original Soul) while living in the world. Moksha is complete freedom from the cycles of birth, death, and rebirth; it is Self-realization. It is the freedom from all limitations of the mind, from limitations of time and space, and from the dependence on artha and kama. Moksha is the realization of our Self as Brahman. This alone is Enlightenment. Anyone can reach this goal. Amma says, "It is possible to reach your spiritual goal while leading a family life, provided you remain detached like a fish in muddy water. Perform your duties toward your family as your duty toward God. In addition to your husband or wife, you should have a friend – and that should be God."

The first three purusharthas are outer goals, whereas the desire for moksha is an inner goal and the true purpose of life. Through knowledge of the impermanent, the desire for the permanent awakens. Eventually the desire for name, fame, and wealth falls away. One does not have to give these things up; one only has to dissolve the attachment to and identification with them. This natural dissolution of old attachments is the first step toward renunciation of the materially focused life in order to reach the goal of moksha. Allowing these attachments and false identifications to fall away is real knowledge. Knowing that nothing is ours and all will pass in time awakens the discerning mind to the temporality of existence.

Amma knows the nature of each of our minds in relation to renunciation. She eloquently explains, "The word 'renunciation' scares some people. Their attitude is that if contentment can come only through giving up, then it is better not to be content. They wonder how they can lead a contented life without wealth, without a beautiful house, a nice car, a wife or husband, without all the conveniences and comforts of life. Without all these, life would be impossible; it would be hell, they think. But do you know anyone whose possessions make them really happy and content? People who look for happiness in life's many conveniences and comforts are the most miserable ones. The more wealth and comforts one has, the more worries and problems one will have. The more one desires, the more one will feel discontent because desires are endless. The chain of greed and selfishness continues to lengthen. It is an endless chain."

When considering the four goals of life, dharma should always come first. We must try to establish our lives in righteousness. Our actions should be motivated by love and compassion instead of selfishness. Then, the proper use of artha and kama will manifest of their own accord. Through life experience, dispassion will arise, and the mind will turn inward. Lasting happiness will come from this inward awareness of the Self.

Ayurveda says that if we can follow these principles, then we can live harmonious, disease-free, healthy lives. Also, if we sincerely follow these guidelines, then we will assist in the restoration of harmony in the world. Sri Adi Shankaracharya said, "What greater fool is there than the one who, having obtained a rare human body, neglects to achieve the real end of this life?"

The ultimate goal of life, Self-realization, should become our primary focus. This precious human birth must not be wasted on sense pleasures and material pursuits alone. Instead, let us use this life to get free from the cycles of birth and death. Now is the only time there is. Turn inward and uncover the truth and beauty that remain hidden deep within.

Ayurveda, naturopathy, yoga, and fasting are invaluable tools that will help us on this journey. When the body and mind have been purified, we will see clearly the nature of the universe and the Self. We must put forth effort for grace to flow. We must strengthen our hearts and minds to be unwavering from the goal. May Amma's grace and love ever bless us.

Let us stand together and show the world that compassion, love, and concern for our fellow beings have not completely vanished from the face of this earth. Let us build a new world of peace and harmony by remaining deeply rooted in the universal values that have nourished humanity since time immemorial. Let us say goodbye to war and brutality forever, reducing them to the stuff of fairytales. Let us be remembered in the future as the generation of peace.

~ Amma